TURKEY

MORE THAN 100 RECIPES
WITH TALES FROM THE ROAD

TURKEY

MORE THAN 100 RECIPES
WITH TALES FROM THE ROAD

Leanne Kitchen

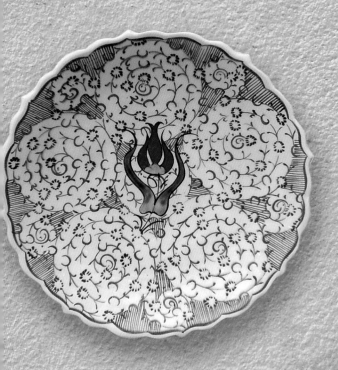

CHRONICLE BOOKS
SAN FRANCISCO

First published in the United States of America in 2012 by Chronicle Books LLC.
First published in Australia in 2011 by Murdoch Books.

Text copyright © 2011 by Leanne Kitchen.
Location photographs copyright © 2011 by Leanne Kitchen.
Food photographs copyright © 2011 by Amanda McLauchlan.

Library of Congress Cataloging-in-Publication Data available.

ISBN 978-1-4521-0770-7

Manufactured in China

Designed by Hugh Ford
Food Styling by Aimee Jones

10 9 8 7 6 5 4 3 2 1

Chronicle Books LLC
680 Second Street
San Francisco, California 94107
www.chroniclebooks.com

CONTENTS

INTRODUCTION 7

MEZE 11

SOUPS 41

BREAD, PASTRY AND PASTA 57

VEGETABLES AND SALADS 89

RICE AND BULGUR 123

FISH AND SEAFOOD 151

POULTRY AND MEAT 185

DESSERTS 227

INDEX 267

ACKNOWLEDGMENTS 272

INTRODUCTION

No matter how exhausted I am after the long flight from Sydney, I start to revive when I see the Istanbul skyline come into view, punctuated as it is by hundreds of minarets and framed by stretches of deep, blue water. There is simply nowhere else on Earth quite like Turkey. By now I know Istanbul well enough to be able to make an instant beeline for my favorite shops, snack stops and restaurants, but I'm still a sucker for many of the city's more clichéd, if defining, charms, such as the müezzin, whose competing calls to prayer from the mosques of Sultanahmet bounce and echo around the ancient cobblestone streets like some sort of sonorous aria.

In common with most Islamic cultures, there's a particular kindness shown to strangers traveling in Turkey. In large and very touristy places like central Istanbul this kindness is not so apparent; although the endless cups of tea offered by those trying to sell something (often a carpet) could be construed as hospitality, albeit with a distinctly commercial edge. The farther off the tourist track I go, the greater the chance I'll be invited to join someone for a snack, or even a home-cooked meal. The tradition of Turkish hospitality forms the perfect framework within which to enjoy the other major reason I so love to come here — the food. Journeying to Turkey, for me, is as much about meeting people and understanding the culture as it is about sharing meals and tasting new flavors.

Every time I disappear into some urban labyrinth or down an isolated village path with a new "friend" I marvel at my willingness to go. After all, that young girl inviting me home for tea could be a kleptomaniac, hell-bent on stealing my credit cards. Those picnicking Kurds are no doubt eyeing me up with white slavery in mind (if you never hear from me again it's because I'm feeding horses, ploughing dirt and hunting with falcons, utterly against my will, somewhere in deepest, darkest Hakkari province). Nothing like this has ever happened of course, but my point is this: I wouldn't be so eager to trot after someone I'd barely met, on the promise of being fed and filled with tea, back home. I'd be considered certifiable.

Turks are extremely proud of their culinary culture and rightly so; it's a rich, varied and venerable cuisine. It is borne of many influences and sources. There are the courtly Ottoman-derived dishes (vestiges of which survive in and around Istanbul and other major centers like Bursa), right through to humble Anatolian peasant fare that speaks of a persistent reliance on the land and the seasons. It produces foodstuffs, ancient in origin, such as yogurts, cheeses and preserved meats, that derive from an earlier, nomadic lifestyle once prevalent throughout Asia Minor. Turkey shares its border with eight nations: Greece, Bulgaria, Georgia, Armenia, Azerbaijan, Iran, Iraq and Syria; all of these have exerted a culinary influence. Until relatively recently, there were significant Greek, Armenian and Jewish communities in the country and their culinary legacy is now so interwoven into the Turkish kitchen vernacular it is impossible to know where one influence ends and another begins.

Modern Turkish cookery is hardly homogenous. Within her borders are seven incredibly diverse regions and not only are these quite distinct culinarily, but within each of the regional borders lie towns, cities and villages which have their own unique dishes, produce and even cooking styles. In Tekirdağ, for example, a town on the Marmara Sea, they make a famous variant of the ubiquitous köfte that's unlike any other. In Edirne, near the border with Bulgaria and Greece, they serve a celebrated liver dish that folk will drive three hours from Istanbul just to eat. From the watermelons of Diyarbakir, the tulum cheese of Erzincan, Isparta rosewater, wheat flour from Konya, Van honey and baldo rice from Tosya to hazelnuts from Giresun, Turkey is a veritable larder of extraordinary produce. And it has a trove of regional dishes that put it to varied and delicious use.

To date, not an awful lot has been documented about regional Turkish cuisine, even within the country. Many Turks are oblivious to the rich culinary diversity on their own doorstep. Little wonder really, as specialties, such as some cheeses and preserves, are made in specific and often far-flung villages and don't get exported further than the nearest large town. Fresh ingredients specific to a region, particularly wild ones like the spring greens of the Aegean, can't readily be found anywhere else.

There are also constants in the general Turkish diet as any visitor to the place will know. Yogurt, kebabs, börek, gözleme, lahmacun, pide and çorba are staples countrywide. In the west of Turkey, particularly in Istanbul, the service of meze is elevated to something of an art form with myriad varieties available. Because of the homogenous nature of much of Turkish restaurant food, and the fact that most of the really interesting stuff gets cooked in the home or on special occasions, digging beyond the standard offerings can be hard. Scoring an invite to eat a home-cooked dinner, or patronizing a restaurant specializing in a specific regional cuisine, are often the only real chances to eat beyond the usual.

My travels through Turkey were fairly random and this is reflected in the recipe content of this book — a collection of some of the best dishes I documented during my travels. Many of these I had researched and sought out, venturing to towns that are well known for their culinary efforts, and others I was fortunate enough to stumble upon by coincidence. I never set out to write the definitive word on Turkish cuisine, but rather let myself be led by the hospitable people of the nation, who were kind enough to share the recipes herein.

MEZE

From a Persian word meaning "pleasant taste," meze refers to a variety of small food items usually served before a main course. Around Istanbul and coastal parts of Turkey, seafood is the main feature, while along the Aegean shoreline, vibrantly flavored local cheeses and wild greens are a favorite. Meze can be as simple as a few lumps of feta, some olives and sliced pastirma, or it can include more elaborate preparations such as stuffed, deep-fried calamari, filled filo pastries or vine leaf rolls stuffed with spice-scented rice. Serve enough meze and you've got an entire meal on your hands. Serve enough raki to go with them, turn up the *fasil* music and you've got a party.

SPICED RED LENTIL KÖFTE

METHOD

Rinse the bulgur under cold running water, then drain well and set aside.

Put the lentils and 2 cups water in a saucepan over medium-low heat. Bring slowly to a simmer, cover, and cook for 15–20 minutes, or until very tender. Remove from the heat and stir in the bulgur. Cover and stand for 15 minutes, or until the mixture is very thick.

Meanwhile, heat the olive oil in a small frying pan over medium-low heat. Add the onion and garlic and cook, stirring often, for 7–8 minutes, or until softened. Add the tomato paste, pepper paste, cumin and paprika and continue stirring for 2–3 minutes, or until fragrant. Stir into the lentil mixture until well combined, then re-cover the pan and set aside until cool.

Once cool, season the lentil mixture with salt and pepper. Mix in the lemon juice and chili powder, using your hands to knead the mixture well and adding a little extra oil or water if the mixture is too dry.

Take 1 tablespoon of mixture at a time and roll into balls, then use your thumb or a finger to make a deep indentation in each. Arrange the köfte balls on a serving plate and drizzle with the extra oil. Serve with the lettuce leaves, scallions, bread and lemon wedges. **SERVES 6**

Note: Turkish pepper paste is a thick red paste made from chilies and salt. It is mainly used as a flavoring, and is available from Middle Eastern and Turkish grocery stores and some delicatessens.

INGREDIENTS

$\frac{3}{4}$ cup fine bulgur

$\frac{3}{4}$ cup red lentils

$2\frac{1}{2}$ tablespoons extra virgin olive oil, plus extra for drizzling

1 large onion, peeled and finely chopped

2 garlic cloves, very finely chopped

1 tablespoon tomato paste

$1\frac{1}{2}$ tablespoons Turkish pepper paste (see note)

$1\frac{1}{2}$ teaspoons ground cumin

$1\frac{1}{2}$ teaspoons paprika

sea salt

freshly ground black pepper

1 tablespoon freshly squeezed lemon juice

1 large pinch chili powder

baby romaine lettuce leaves, to serve

4 scallions, roots removed and trimmed, to serve

Turkish bread or flat bread (page 63), to serve

lemon wedges, to serve

SMOKY EGGPLANT, CARROT AND CARAWAY, AND BEET AND YOGURT DIPS

SMOKY EGGPLANT DIP

3 eggplants

$\frac{1}{3}$ cup extra virgin olive oil

2 garlic cloves, crushed

$2\frac{1}{2}$ tablespoons freshly squeezed lemon
    juice, or to taste

1 cup Greek yogurt

sea salt

freshly ground black pepper

CARROT AND CARAWAY DIP

$2\frac{1}{2}$ tablespoons extra virgin olive oil

4 carrots, grated

$\frac{1}{2}$ teaspoon caraway seeds

1 cup Greek yogurt

sea salt

freshly ground black pepper

BEET AND YOGURT DIP

3 beets, trimmed

$2\frac{1}{2}$ tablespoons extra virgin olive oil,
    plus extra for brushing

2 garlic cloves

1 cup Greek yogurt

sea salt

freshly ground black pepper

crisp lavash or flat bread (page 63),
    to serve

SMOKY EGGPLANT DIP

Place the eggplants directly over a low flame and cook for about 20 minutes, turning often, until the skin is blackened all over and the centers are soft. (Alternatively, cook the eggplants on a barbecue grill heated to high.) Transfer the eggplants to a large bowl and cool slightly. When cool enough to handle, peel off the skins, removing as much of the blackened skin as possible, and trim the stem end. Transfer the flesh to a colander and drain for about 20 minutes to remove any excess liquid.

Transfer the eggplant to a large bowl and use a fork to mash well. Add the olive oil, garlic, lemon juice and yogurt and stir well to combine. Season with salt and pepper.

CARROT AND CARAWAY DIP

Heat the oil in a saucepan over medium-low heat. Add the carrot, cover, and cook for 20 minutes, stirring often, until the carrot is very tender. Remove from the heat and cool to room temperature. Add the caraway seeds and yogurt, season with salt and pepper and stir well to combine.

BEET AND YOGURT DIP

Preheat the oven to 350°F. Brush each beet with a little olive oil to coat, then individually wrap them in foil and place in a small roasting tin. Roast the beets for 1 hour 40 minutes, or until tender. Remove from the oven and cool to room temperature.

Grate the beets into a large bowl or cut into $\frac{1}{4}$-inch cubes and combine with the olive oil, garlic and yogurt, stirring well to combine; season with salt and pepper.

These dips can be stored in an airtight container in the refrigerator for up to 2 days. Bring back to room temperature and stir well before serving with the lavash. **SERVES 6**

At its very essence Turkish food is incredibly simple. While there are complex dishes in the country's culinary lexicon, it's dishes such as this one that stand out. A humble ingredient such as the leek is treated in such a way as to taste truly and deeply of itself.

LEEKS WITH LEMON, CURRANTS AND TULUM

METHOD

Preheat the oven to 350°F. For baby leeks, pull off any tough outer layers and trim $1\frac{1}{4}$–$1\frac{1}{2}$ inches from the tops. Trim the roots, taking care to leave the root ends intact or they will fall apart during cooking. For large leeks, trim and discard the green part of the leeks and any long roots, then cut in half lengthwise. Soak the leeks in clean water, taking care to remove all the dirt trapped between the layers. Place in a single layer in a large roasting pan.

Heat the olive oil in a small saucepan over medium-low heat. Add the garlic and cook for 2 minutes, or until fragrant. Pour the oil mixture over the leeks in the pan. Scatter the sugar, lemon zest, thyme and currants over the leeks, then pour the lemon juice and stock into the roasting pan; season with pepper. Cover the pan tightly with foil and bake for about 25 minutes for baby leeks, or 50 minutes for the large ones — the leeks will be tender when done. Remove from the oven, drain the leeks and set aside, reserving the cooking liquid. Remove the thyme.

Transfer the reserved cooking liquid to a saucepan over high heat and bring to a boil. Cook for 10 minutes, or until the liquid has reduced and thickened, then pour over the leeks. Season with salt and cool. Once cool, transfer to a serving dish, scatter over the crumbled tulum cheese and serve. **SERVES 4**

Note: Tulum cheese is a white, crumbly sheep's milk cheese that is traditionally aged in a "bag" made from the hide of the animal. Strong and pleasantly sharp in flavor, you can find it if you are lucky enough to live near a Middle Eastern or Turkish grocery store. Feta is a fine substitute if tulum cheese is unavailable.

INGREDIENTS

2 bunches baby leeks or 4 large leeks

$\frac{1}{2}$ cup extra virgin olive oil

2 garlic cloves, thinly sliced

$2\frac{1}{2}$ teaspoons superfine sugar

finely grated zest of 1 lemon

2 thyme sprigs

$\frac{1}{4}$ cup currants

$\frac{1}{4}$ cup freshly squeezed lemon juice

$1\frac{1}{2}$ cups chicken stock

freshly ground black pepper

sea salt

$4\frac{1}{2}$ oz tulum cheese (see note), crumbled

The roots of this meze classic lie in Georgian cooking (walnuts are a big feature of that cuisine). In Turkey it's served doused in sauce, although I've lightened the effect here and added a few greens. Use the freshest walnuts you can find. This dish tastes even better the next day but bring it to room temperature before serving.

CHICKEN AND WALNUT SALAD

INGREDIENTS

3 lb 5 oz whole free-range chicken

1 carrot

1 onion

2 celery sticks

1 fresh bay leaf

1 teaspoon whole allspice berries

1 cinnamon stick

about 4 slices day-old rustic bread,
     crusts removed

3 garlic cloves, chopped

2 cups walnut halves

$\frac{1}{2}$ cup olive oil

$2\frac{1}{2}$ teaspoons red wine vinegar, or to taste

$\frac{1}{2}$ cup whole egg mayonnaise

1 teaspoon dried chili flakes, or to taste,
     plus extra to serve

$2\frac{1}{2}$ teaspoons sweet paprika

sea salt

freshly ground black pepper

3 scallions, trimmed and cut into long strips

4 cups watercress sprigs

METHOD

Put the whole chicken into a large saucepan with the carrot, onion, celery, bay leaf, allspice and cinnamon stick and add just enough cold water to cover. Cover with a lid and bring to a gentle simmer over medium-low heat for 45 minutes — do not let the water boil or the chicken will be tough. When the chicken is tender, remove from the liquid and cool to room temperature. Strain the cooking liquid, discarding the solids. Skim any fat from the surface of the liquid and reserve. Remove the chicken flesh from the bones, discarding the skin and bones and breaking the flesh into coarse chunks. Set aside.

Soak the bread in water for 1–2 minutes, then use your hands to squeeze out as much water as possible. Combine in a food processor with the garlic, walnuts, olive oil and vinegar and process until a coarse paste forms. Add the mayonnaise, chili flakes, paprika and $\frac{1}{2}$ cup of the reserved cooking liquid and process until the mixture is smooth, thick and creamy, adding a little more cooking liquid if needed. Season with salt and pepper and a little more vinegar, to taste.

Place the scallions into a bowl of iced water and stand for 3–4 minutes, or until curled slightly, then drain well. Toss in a bowl with the watercress and divide among serving plates. Combine the chicken in a bowl with just enough of the walnut sauce to lightly coat. Pile on top of the watercress and sprinkle with extra chili flakes, to taste. Serve immediately with the remaining sauce passed separately. **SERVES 4–6**

DIKKAT!
SATICI ve DİLENCİ
GİREMEZ

EMİNÖNÜ
YENİCAMİİ
1597 — 1663
NEW MOSQUE

A MORNING IN ISTANBUL

It's tricky to narrow down my favorite food experience in a city as large and diverse as Istanbul, but if I had just one morning there, based on the many times I've visited, this is most likely how I'd spend it.

I'd breakfast in the same, no-frills place around the corner from the Hippodrome in Sultanahmet where I always go. It's nothing special, just a workers' canteen really, but I like the poğaça. Afterward, I'd follow the light rail track past the old train station that is still in use and was once the terminus for the fabled *Orient Express*. At the food market near the glorious Yeni Cami (or "new" mosque), vendors arrive early to set up their shops with spices, cheese, vine leaves and pickles, nuts, pastirma and sujuk. It's a good place for a scratch-and-sniff foray — I'd taste tulum cheese from Erzurum, still in its goat-hide casing; minci, a salty cheese from Trabzon; the finest pastirma from Kayseri; and sweet jam from Kastamonu, famous for its wild strawberries. Even with a stomach lined with breakfast, I can never say no.

Next, I'd skip behind the spice bazaar to the warren of streets filled with copper and candy shops, textile stores and men peddling cartloads of cucumbers or simit and walk over the Galata Bridge toward the retail melee along Istiklal Caddesi, with its Mavi jean boutiques, bookshops, bars and cafés. A quick diversion to Karaköy Güllüoğlu, which claims to make "the best baklava in Istanbul," is of course on the agenda. I'd never argue — these guys are from Gaziantep and know a thing or two about baklava. Tanked-up on their syrupy squares of deliciousness, I'd wend my way up to Cihangir where the skinny streets are lined with old European-style apartment buildings and antique shops. It's not hard to lose hours rummaging around here so there's no point keeping time.

When my stomach tells me to move on, I'm perfectly poised to drop into Antiocha, a little place run by a friend who hails from the southern town of Antakya near the Syrian border, where the food is legendary. The menu is small but well edited and makes a feature of boutique-produced olive oil, cheeses and olives from Antakya, homemade yogurt and the best beef money can buy. Rarely is shish kebab as juicy and succulent, and the wonderfully flavored meze (such as *kekik salatasi*, a relish-like assemblage of olives, thyme and olive oil) are veritable flavor explosions.

But then this is Istanbul, so you'll definitely need more than one morning to truly make the most of it.

OCTOPUS WITH POTATOES, OLIVES AND ORANGE-PAPRIKA VINAIGRETTE

ORANGE-PAPRIKA VINAIGRETTE

1 orange, peel removed in large strips,
    white pith removed, and cut into
    very fine julienne
2 cups freshly squeezed orange juice
2 tablespoons freshly squeezed lemon juice
$1\frac{1}{2}$ teaspoons sweet paprika
2 teaspoons dijon mustard
2 teaspoons sugar
sea salt
freshly ground black pepper
$\frac{1}{2}$ cup extra virgin olive oil

3 lb 5 oz octopus, cleaned
4 oregano sprigs
1 fresh bay leaf
2 garlic cloves, bruised
$1\frac{1}{2}$ teaspoons whole allspice berries
1 lemon, halved widthwise
1 lb 5 oz waxy potatoes, peeled
$\frac{2}{3}$ cup small black olives
$\frac{1}{2}$ cup cilantro sprigs, to serve

ORANGE-PAPRIKA VINAIGRETTE

Combine the orange zest and juice in a small saucepan and bring to a boil. Reduce the heat to medium-low and simmer for about 30 minutes, or until the liquid has reduced by about half. Remove from the heat and cool. Whisk the cooled orange reduction with the lemon juice, paprika, mustard and sugar. Add the olive oil in a slow steady stream, whisking constantly. Season with salt and pepper. Set aside until ready to serve.

Place the octopus in a saucepan with the oregano, bay leaf, garlic, allspice and 1 cup water. Squeeze the lemon halves to extract the juice, then strain, reserving the skins. Add the juice and lemon halves to the pan. Cover with a tight-fitting lid and cook over medium-low heat for $1\frac{1}{2}$ hours, or until the octopus is very tender and any large suckers easily pull off. Drain the octopus, discarding the lemon halves, herbs and allspice; cool. Pull the large suckers and any thick skin off the octopus; remove the tentacles from the bodies (they will just tear off). Cut the octopus bodies into $\frac{1}{2}$-inch pieces and tentacles into smaller pieces and set aside.

Meanwhile, cook the potatoes in salted boiling water for 7–8 minutes, or until just tender. Drain well, cool to room temperature then cut widthwise into $\frac{1}{2}$-inch-thick slices. Combine in a bowl with the octopus and olives; season with salt and pepper. Drizzle over the dressing and toss well to combine, then divide among bowls or pile onto a large platter. Scatter the cilantro over and serve immediately. **SERVES 6**

FAVA BEAN PURÉE WITH EGG SALAD

FAVA BEAN PURÉE

$1\frac{1}{2}$ cups whole dried fava beans

1 brown onion, finely chopped

1 all-purpose potato, peeled
    and chopped

$1\frac{1}{2}$ cups podded and peeled fresh
    or frozen fava beans

3 teaspoons sugar

2 tablespoons extra virgin olive oil,
    plus extra to serve

sea salt

freshly ground black pepper

EGG SALAD

$2\frac{1}{2}$ tablespoons freshly squeezed
    lemon juice, or to taste

1 teaspoon finely grated lemon zest

$\frac{1}{2}$ cup extra virgin olive oil

4 hard-boiled eggs, peeled and coarsely
    chopped

$\frac{1}{3}$ cup sun-dried tomatoes, cut into
    thick strips

2 tablespoons chopped fresh dill

2 cups watercress sprigs

grilled Turkish bread, to serve

FAVA BEAN PURÉE

Put the dried beans in a bowl, cover with cold water and leave to soak overnight. Drain well, then remove and discard the skins. Put the beans, onion and potato in a saucepan over medium heat and add just enough water to barely cover; bring slowly to a simmer. Reduce the heat to low and cook for 40 minutes, adding a little extra water if necessary (do not add too much water or the finished purée will not be firm enough). Stir in the fresh or frozen fava beans and continue cooking for 15 minutes, or until the beans are tender. Remove from the heat and cool slightly.

Transfer the bean mixture to a food processor. Add the sugar and olive oil and process to make a smooth purée. Season with salt and pepper. Place in a well-oiled 4-cup-capacity terrine mold or loaf pan, smoothing the surface with the back of a spoon. Cool to room temperature, then cover and refrigerate for 2–3 hours or overnight.

EGG SALAD

To make the egg salad, combine the lemon juice, lemon zest and olive oil in a bowl and whisk well to combine. Add the egg, sun-dried tomato, dill and watercress and toss to combine, being careful not to break up the egg too much.

To serve, turn the purée out onto a platter and spoon over the egg salad. Drizzle with olive oil and serve with the grilled Turkish bread passed separately. **SERVES 6**

MUHAMARA WITH STUFFED FLAT BREAD

MUHAMARA

Place the bell peppers directly over a low flame and cook for about 10–15 minutes, turning often, until the skin is blackened all over. (Alternatively, cook the bell peppers on a barbecue grill heated to high.) Transfer to a bowl, cover with a tea towel (dish towel) and stand until cool enough to handle. Remove the blackened skins and seeds — do not rinse them with water or you will lose flavor. Tear the bell pepper into pieces and combine in a food processor with the remaining ingredients to make a coarse paste. Season with salt and pepper, then transfer to a bowl, cover with plastic wrap and refrigerate for at least 8 hours for the flavors to develop. Muhamara can be stored in an airtight container in the refrigerator for 4–5 days.

STUFFED FLAT BREAD

Combine the sugar and ⅔ cup lukewarm water in a small bowl, then sprinkle over the yeast. Set aside for about 8 minutes, or until foamy, then add another ⅓ cup lukewarm water and the olive oil.

Combine the flours and the salt in a bowl, add the yeast mixture, and stir to form a coarse dough. Turn out onto a lightly floured board and knead for 7–8 minutes, or until the dough is smooth and elastic. Cover with plastic wrap and set aside in a warm, draft-free place for 1 hour, or until doubled in size.

Meanwhile combine the feta, olives and oregano in a bowl to make the filling.

Knock back the dough on a lightly floured surface and use a large knife to divide the dough into 12 even-sized pieces. Working with one piece of dough at a time, use a rolling pin to roll each piece into a rough circle with a 5½-inch diameter. Divide the filling between the rounds and use your fingers to bring the edges over the top to enclose the filling and form a ball. Place each ball on a floured surface, seam side down, then gently roll out with a rolling pin to make a circle with a 4–4½-inch diameter.

Heat a heavy-based frying pan over low heat and brush the base with a little of the extra olive oil. Cook the flat breads, one or two at a time, for 3–4 minutes on each side, or until a deep golden color and cooked through.

Serve the muhamara at room temperature with the extra olive oil drizzled over and sprinkled with pistachios (if using), and warm flat bread on the side.
SERVES 6–8

Note: Pomegranate molasses features in the cooking of southern Turkey where a distinct Middle Eastern influence runs strong. It is made from the boiled-down juice of pomegranates and has a wonderful sweet-tart flavor quite unlike anything else. It is available from most large supermarkets.

MUHAMARA

4 large red bell peppers
3 slices day-old rustic bread, cut into small pieces
1 garlic clove, chopped
1¼ cups walnut halves, coarsely chopped
1 large pinch dried chili flakes
1 tablespoon tomato paste
2 teaspoons freshly squeezed lemon juice
2 tablespoons pomegranate molasses (see note)
1½ teaspoons superfine sugar
1 teaspoon ground cumin
2 tablespoons olive oil, plus extra to serve
sea salt
freshly ground black pepper
chopped pistachios to serve (optional)

STUFFED FLAT BREAD

1 teaspoon sugar
1½ teaspoons instant dried yeast
1½ tablespoons olive oil, plus extra for cooking
2 cups all-purpose flour, sifted
1 cup whole-wheat flour, sifted
1 teaspoon sea salt
1 cup crumbled feta cheese
1 cup pitted green olives, chopped
¼ cup oregano leaves

ALBANIAN LIVER WITH ONION AND PAPRIKA SAUCE

ONION AND PAPRIKA SAUCE

Heat the olive oil in a large, heavy-based saucepan over medium heat. Add the onion and cook, stirring often, for 12–15 minutes, or until very soft. Add the currants and paprika, stirring well, and cook for 1–2 minutes. Add the sugar, vinegar and stock and bring to a simmer, then reduce the heat to low and cook for 20 minutes, or until the onion is very tender and the liquid has reduced. Season with salt and pepper.

Cut the liver into $\frac{1}{2}$-inch-thick strips. Combine the flour, paprika and chili powder in a bowl and season well. Add the liver and toss to coat. Heat half of the oil in a large, heavy-based frying pan over medium-high heat. Add half of the liver and cook for 3–4 minutes, turning once, or until golden and cooked through but still a little pink in the middle. Remove to a plate lined with baking paper and keep warm. Repeat with the remaining oil and liver until cooked. Serve immediately with the sauce on the side. **SERVES 6**

ONION AND PAPRIKA SAUCE

$\frac{1}{4}$ cup extra virgin olive oil

1 lb 12 oz onions, peeled and thinly sliced

$\frac{1}{4}$ cup currants

2 teaspoons sweet paprika

1 tablespoon superfine sugar

$\frac{1}{4}$ cup cider vinegar

$1\frac{1}{4}$ cups chicken stock

sea salt

freshly ground black pepper

1 lb 10 oz lamb or veal livers, trimmed
    and fine membrane removed

$\frac{1}{2}$ cup all-purpose flour

2 teaspoons sweet paprika

1 teaspoon chili powder, or to taste

$\frac{1}{3}$ cup extra virgin olive oil

WARM SQUASH HUMMUS

METHOD

Put the drained chickpeas in a saucepan with enough fresh water to cover. Cook in simmering water for 1 hour, or until very tender. Drain well and cool slightly. Using your hands, rub the chickpeas vigorously to loosen the skins, then remove as many skins as possible (this step may seem fussy but will greatly improve the texture of the hummus).

Meanwhile, heat the oil in a saucepan over medium heat. Add the squash, cover, and cook for 20–25 minutes, stirring occasionally, until the squash is very tender. Put the hot squash and any cooking juices in a food processor with the chickpeas, garlic, lemon juice and tahini and process until the mixture is well combined and smooth. Season with salt, pepper and dried chili flakes (if using), then serve immediately. **SERVES 6**

INGREDIENTS

$1\frac{1}{4}$ cups dried chickpeas, soaked
    overnight and drained

$\frac{1}{4}$ cup extra virgin olive oil

1 lb 5 oz butternut squash,
    peeled, seeded and chopped

2 garlic cloves, crushed

$\frac{1}{4}$ cup freshly squeezed lemon
    juice, or to taste

$2\frac{1}{2}$ tablespoons tahini

sea salt

freshly ground black pepper

dried chili flakes, to taste (optional)

BREAKFAST IN VAN

The first time I waddled happily out of the Van Kahvalti Evi (Van Breakfast House) in trendy Cihangir in Istanbul, a restaurant making a feature of the celebrated breakfast foods of Van, I determined to visit that far-flung city near the border with Iran as soon as possible. As I bus in from Doğubeyazit to the north, we start skirting the mighty, azure Lake Van, sparkling with more shades of blue than I knew existed. There's a spectacular show of wildflowers along the shore (it's spring), dramatic snow-capped mountains to the south, itinerant bee keepers camped along the roadside and a highway frequently reduced to a crawl by flocks of herding sheep. Upon first appearances the town itself seems bland and utilitarian, but the longer I stay (and the more I return), the more Van grows on me. The atmosphere is friendly and laid-back. I always have a great time in Van but it is without doubt the breakfasts that keep me coming back.

Breakfasting is taken so seriously in Van there is even a street, Kahvalti Caddesi (Breakfast Street), devoted to its consumption. Typically, the eateries' windows are littered with tubs of glistening olives, neat chunks of gooey honeycomb, elegant folds of *kaymak* (Turkish clotted cream that in these parts is made from sheep's milk), mounds of rich local butter and some interesting variations on a theme of cheese. Included in this is the fabled *otlu peynir*, or "grassy cheese," so-called on account of the chopped wild mountain herbs that are incorporated into the piquant, white curd. Locals tank up on "the works," which includes plates of all of the above, plus boiled eggs, wedges of tomato, slices of cucumber and mountains of *ekmek*, a crusty, chewy bread delivered hot from the nearby bakehouse. Hungrier souls order *murtuğa*, eggs scrambled with butter and flour, or *kavut*, a local specialty made by toasting coarse wholemeal flour, then cooking it to a thick porridge with butter, milk and sugar. I've learned to edit my breakfast down to a few, mind-blowing basics and my breakfast of choice involves chewy bread, *kaymak* and honey.

The Turkish word for breakfast, *kahvalti*, means "before coffee," so tulip-shaped glasses of strong sweet tea are the thing to accompany morning food. Tea and an overly loud television blasting out the latest Galatasaray, Beştiktaş or Fernerbahce victory to all who care. In this soccer-crazed nation, all (except me) care deeply. Even at breakfast time.

Strictly speaking, this is more of a breakfast dish than a meze but you could easily serve it as a meze by omitting the eggs. If you can't find sujuk, a wonderfully spicy, dry Turkish sausage, you can substitute a not-too-hot merguez or chorizo instead.

SPICY LENTILS BAKED WITH EGGS AND SUJUK

METHOD

Put the lentils in a saucepan and add enough cold water to just cover. Bring to a simmer and cook for 10 minutes, or until partially cooked. Drain well and set aside.

Heat half the olive oil in a saucepan over medium heat. Add the onion, carrot, celery, garlic, bay leaves and cinnamon, and cook for 6–7 minutes, or until the onion has softened. Add the paprika, chili flakes and tomato paste and cook, stirring, for 1–2 minutes, or until fragrant. Add the tomatoes, stock and par-cooked lentils and stir well to combine. Bring to a simmer, cover, then reduce the heat to low and cook for 20 minutes, or until the lentils are tender. Season with salt and pepper. Discard the cinnamon stick and bay leaves.

Preheat the oven to 350°F. Divide the lentil mixture between four 2½-cup ovenproof baking dishes. Break two eggs into each dish over the lentil mixture and bake for 15–20 minutes, or until the eggs are set.

Meanwhile, heat the remaining oil in a large frying pan over medium heat. Add slices of sujuk to the pan and cook for 3–4 minutes on each side, or until golden. Divide among the dishes and serve immediately. **SERVES 4**

Note: Red Persian lentils are small and nutty in flavor, and much like puy lentils they hold their shape perfectly when cooked. They are available from specialty grocery stores. You can use ordinary brown lentils if red Persian lentils are unavailable.

INGREDIENTS

1¼ cups red Persian lentils
   (see note) or brown lentils

⅓ cup olive oil

1 large onion, finely chopped

1 carrot, peeled and finely chopped

1 celery stick, finely chopped

3 garlic cloves, finely chopped

2 fresh bay leaves

1 cinnamon stick

2 teaspoons sweet paprika

1 teaspoon dried chili flakes, or to taste

2 tablespoons tomato paste

3¼ cups canned chopped tomatoes

2 cups chicken stock

sea salt

freshly ground black pepper

8 eggs

1 lb 5 oz sujuk (Turkish sausage), cut
   into ½-inch-thick slices

CABBAGE, SHRIMP AND RICE DOLMAS

INGREDIENTS

1 green cabbage

½ cup long-grain white rice

3 lb raw king shrimp, peeled, deveined and chopped

1 onion, very finely chopped

2 garlic cloves, finely chopped

2 tablespoons tomato paste

⅓ cup small capers, drained

1 teaspoon paprika

2½ tablespoons chopped Italian parsley

2½ tablespoons chopped fresh dill

sea salt

freshly ground black pepper

2 cups chicken stock

extra virgin olive oil, to serve

chopped fresh dill, to serve

lemon wedges, to serve

METHOD

Discard the tough outer cabbage leaves. Carefully remove the large outer cabbage leaves, cutting in half along the central vein — you need about 12 leaves in total. Bring a large saucepan of salted water to a boil and blanch the leaves, in batches, for 3 minutes each, or until softened. Drain well and set aside to cool; pat dry with paper towels to remove any excess liquid.

Soak the rice in a bowl of cold water for 10 minutes, then drain well. Combine in a bowl with the chopped shrimp, onion, garlic, tomato paste, capers, paprika, parsley and dill. Season with salt and pepper, then use your hands to mix everything together.

Cut each half cabbage leaf in half. Working with one piece at a time, place on a work surface with a long edge facing towards you. Place a heaped tablespoon of the rice mixture along the edge, leaving a slight border, then fold the shorter edges over and roll up into a finger, about 1½ inches long — don't roll the dolmas too tightly as they need a little room to expand. You may not need all of the cabbage leaves.

Use the remaining leaves to line a saucepan large enough to fit the dolmas in a single layer. Arrange the dolmas carefully in the pan, seam side down. Pour over the stock. Place a plate over the dolmas to keep them slightly weighted down, then cover the pan with a lid. Place over medium heat, bring to a simmer, then reduce the heat to low and cook for 1 hour. Remove the pan from the heat and cool the dolmas slightly. When cool enough to handle, carefully remove the dolmas from the pan and cool to room temperature. Serve with the olive oil drizzled over the top and scatter the dill and the lemon wedges on the side. **MAKES ABOUT 30**

I can't say I ate green tomatoes and celery prepared this way in Turkey, but the zingy flavors are a perfect foil for fried cheese, which I did enjoy on the Aegean coast. In these parts, the food is influenced by neighboring Greece — although any Turk will tell you that *they* taught the Greeks to cook.

FRIED HALOUMI WITH GREEN TOMATO AND CELERY RELISH

GREEN TOMATO AND CELERY RELISH

Heat the olive oil in a saucepan over medium heat. Add the onion and garlic and cook for 5 minutes, or until softened. Add the tomato, celery, capers and cinnamon, cover, and cook for 5 minutes, stirring occasionally until the tomatoes have softened slightly and released some juices. Add the honey, vinegar and allspice, bring back to a simmer and cook, uncovered, for 10 minutes. Remove from the heat, cool to room temperature, then season with salt and pepper. Remove the cinnamon stick and set the relish aside until ready to serve.

Just before you are ready to serve, cook the haloumi. Heat the oil in a large frying pan over medium heat. Dust the haloumi lightly in the seasoned flour, shaking off any excess. Add to the pan in a single layer and cook, in batches if necessary, for 3 minutes on each side or until golden. Divide among warmed plates or arrange on a platter with the lemon wedges. Serve the relish on the side and scatter with the dill. **SERVES 6**

GREEN TOMATO AND CELERY RELISH

$2\frac{1}{2}$ tablespoons extra virgin olive oil

2 onions, very finely chopped

3 garlic cloves, finely sliced

1 lb 5 oz green tomatoes, cut into
$\frac{1}{2}$-inch pieces

2 celery sticks, cut on the diagonal into
$\frac{1}{4}$-inch-thick slices

$\frac{1}{4}$ cup capers, drained

1 cinnamon stick

$1\frac{1}{2}$ tablespoons honey

2 tablespoons white wine vinegar

1 teaspoon ground allspice

sea salt

freshly ground black pepper

$2\frac{1}{2}$ tablespoons chopped fresh dill

1 lb 5 oz haloumi, sliced into
$\frac{1}{2}$-inch-thick pieces

$\frac{1}{4}$ cup olive oil

seasoned flour, for dusting

lemon wedges, to serve

LITTLE FISH MARINATED IN VINEGAR, TOMATO, OREGANO AND ALLSPICE

INGREDIENTS

2 lb 12 oz whole skinless, boneless mackerel
    or whiting, cleaned and patted dry
plain (all-purpose) flour, for dusting
olive oil, for frying
1 cup red wine vinegar
1 cup tomato passata
    (puréed tomatoes)
2 cups extra virgin olive oil
$\frac{1}{4}$ cup honey
4 dried oregano sprigs
6 garlic cloves, bruised
1 teaspoon ground allspice
sea salt
freshly ground black pepper

METHOD

Dust the fish lightly in the flour, shaking off any excess. Heat a little olive oil in a large, heavy-based frying pan over medium heat. Cook the fish, in batches, for 2–3 minutes on each side, or until just cooked through. Remove to a tray while cooking the remaining fish, adding more oil to the pan as needed.

Combine the vinegar, tomato passata, extra virgin olive oil, honey, oregano, garlic and allspice in a saucepan and slowly bring to a simmer. Reduce the heat to low and cook for 2–3 minutes, then remove from the heat and cool slightly.

Arrange the fish in a large ceramic dish, season well with salt and pepper and pour over the vinegar mixture. Cool to room temperature, cover with plastic wrap and refrigerate overnight. Bring to room temperature to serve. **SERVES 6-8**

TUNA IN OLIVE OIL

INGREDIENTS

1 lb 12 oz tuna steaks, blood
    line trimmed
2 teaspoons coriander seeds
$1\frac{1}{2}$ teaspoons cumin seeds
1 tablespoon superfine sugar
1 tablespoon sea salt
1 lemon
1 teaspoon freshly ground black pepper
$1\frac{1}{2}$ cups extra virgin olive oil

METHOD

Using a sharp knife, cut the tuna steaks on a slight diagonal into pieces about $1\frac{1}{2}$ inches wide. Toast the coriander and cumin seeds in a dry small, heavy-based frying pan over medium-low heat for 2–3 minutes, shaking the pan occasionally, or until fragrant. Coarsely grind the spices using a mortar and pestle or an electric spice grinder.

Generously oil the base and sides of a $10\frac{1}{2}$-x-6-inch ceramic or glass dish. Arrange the fish in a single layer so they slightly overlap and sprinkle over the spices, sugar and salt. Cover with plastic wrap and let stand at room temperature for 30 minutes.

Meanwhile, preheat the oven to 250°F. Finely grate the lemon and sprinkle the zest over the tuna. Squeeze and strain the lemon juice, then pour over the tuna. Add the pepper and drizzle with the olive oil — it should just cover the fish. Cover the dish tightly with foil and bake for about 30 minutes, or until the tuna is just cooked through. Remove from the oven and allow to cool in the oil; serve at room temperature. The tuna will keep, stored in the oil, covered and refrigerated, for up to 5 days. **SERVES 6-8**

SOUPS

It's fair to say Turks love soups. They can literally start and end the day with a soup. Lentil soup (*mercimek çorbası*) is a beloved, and fortifying, breakfast staple, which often gets wolfed down on the run accompanied by handfuls of crusty bread. Tripe soup (*işkembe çorbası*) is a late-night favorite used to revive tired bodies from an evening of heavy partying. Turkish soups are generally light and simple affairs that make a feature of just one or two main ingredients — think rice and tomato, a selection of fish, or yogurt and barley.

Yogurt is a Turkish staple — indeed, it is a Turkish word. It is used in soups, as it is here, and served alongside kebabs, köfte and other meat dishes, also forming the basis of many dips and spreads. A liaison of egg yolk and lemon juice is a typical addition to a Turkish soup, thickening the liquid and adding a silky richness.

YOGURT, MINT AND BARLEY SOUP

METHOD

Put the barley, bay leaf and stock in a saucepan over medium-low heat and bring to a simmer. Partially cover the pan and cook for 30 minutes, or until the barley is tender.

Combine the yogurt, dried mint, egg yolks and lemon zest in a bowl and whisk well to combine. In a separate smaller bowl, mix together the cornstarch and lemon juice to form a smooth paste. Stir the cornstarch mixture into the yogurt mixture. Use a ladle to transfer about 2 cups of the hot stock mixture into the yogurt mixture and stir to combine well. Pour this back into the stock in the pan, then, stirring constantly, continue to cook the soup over medium heat until it just comes back to a simmer and thickens. Serve immediately sprinkled with some lemon zest. **SERVES 4-6**

INGREDIENTS

$\frac{1}{2}$ cup pearl barley

1 fresh bay leaf

4 cups chicken stock

2 cups Greek yogurt

2 teaspoons dried mint

3 egg yolks

2 teaspoons finely grated lemon zest, plus extra to serve

1 tablespoon cornstarch

$2\frac{1}{2}$ tablespoons freshly squeezed lemon juice

LENTIL, SWISS CHARD AND LAMB KÖFTE SOUP

INGREDIENTS

1 cup dried chickpeas, soaked
  overnight and drained

KÖFTE

$\frac{1}{2}$ cup fine bulgur

$\frac{1}{2}$ cup all-purpose flour

7 oz ground lamb

$2\frac{1}{2}$ teaspoons tomato paste

$\frac{1}{2}$ teaspoon ground allspice

$\frac{1}{2}$ teaspoon ground cinnamon

sea salt

freshly ground black pepper

$\frac{1}{4}$ cup olive oil

2 onions, finely chopped

3 garlic cloves, crushed

2 tablespoons tomato paste

2 tablespoons Turkish pepper paste
  (see note page 13)

$2\frac{1}{2}$ teaspoons dried oregano

1 fresh bay leaf

$1\frac{1}{3}$ cups brown lentils

$2\frac{1}{2}$ quarts chicken stock

1 bunch Swiss chard, trimmed,
  stems and ribs removed and leaves
  finely chopped

lemon wedges, to serve

Greek yogurt, to serve

dried chili flakes, to serve

extra virgin olive oil, to serve

METHOD

Put the chickpeas in a saucepan with just enough water to cover. Bring to a boil, then reduce the heat to low and simmer for 1 hour, or until tender. Drain the chickpeas, cover and reserve.

KÖFTE

Rinse the bulgur and drain well, using your hands to squeeze out as much excess liquid as possible. Combine in a food processor with the flour, lamb, tomato paste, allspice and cinnamon; season with salt and pepper. Process until the mixture is smooth and elastic. Take scant teaspoonfuls of the mixture at a time and roll into neat balls using your hands. Place on a baking sheet lined with parchment paper and refrigerate until needed.

Heat the olive oil in a large saucepan over medium heat. Add the onion and garlic and cook for 5–6 minutes, or until softened. Add the tomato paste, pepper paste, oregano and bay leaf and cook, stirring, for another 1 minute. Add the lentils and chicken stock, bring to a boil, then reduce the heat to low and simmer for 50 minutes, or until the lentils are tender. Add the chickpeas and cook for 3–4 minutes to heat through, then stir in the Swiss chard. Bring the soup back to a gentle simmer and carefully stir in the köfte; cook over low heat for 6–7 minutes, or until the chard has wilted and the köfte are cooked through. Season with salt and pepper and serve the soup in large bowls with the lemon wedges, yogurt, chili flakes and olive oil passed separately. **SERVES 6**

TOMATO, BELL PEPPER AND RICE SOUP WITH GOAT'S CURD AND CILANTRO

INGREDIENTS

2 lb 4 oz very ripe tomatoes, chopped

$2\frac{1}{2}$ tablespoons extra virgin olive oil, plus extra to serve

1 onion, finely chopped

2 garlic cloves, crushed

2 large red bell peppers, seeded, ribs removed and finely chopped

$1\frac{1}{2}$ tablespoons Turkish pepper paste (see note page 13)

$\frac{1}{2}$ teaspoon dried chili flakes, or to taste

2 teaspoons sweet paprika

$\frac{1}{3}$ cup medium-grain rice

1 tablespoon sugar

$2\frac{1}{2}$ cups chicken stock

sea salt

freshly ground black pepper

$4\frac{1}{2}$ oz goat's curd

chopped cilantro leaves, to serve

METHOD

Put the tomato into a food processor and process until a smooth purée forms.

Heat the olive oil in a large saucepan over medium heat. Add the onion and garlic and cook for 5–6 minutes, or until softened. Add the bell peppers and cook for 10 minutes, stirring often, until softened. Add the pepper paste, chili flakes and paprika and cook, stirring, for 1 minute, then add the rice, sugar, chicken stock and tomato purée and stir well to combine. Bring to a simmer, then cook over medium-low heat for 20 minutes, or until the rice is very tender. Season with salt and pepper. Divide among serving bowls. Divide the goat's curd among the bowls, sprinkle with the cilantro, drizzle with a little extra olive oil and serve immediately. **SERVES 4-6**

Turkey is the third-largest producer of pistachios in the world. The fattest, greenest, sweetest nuts are grown around the southern Turkish city of Gaziantep. Large piles and sacks of nuts are on display at the local markets, available in all sizes and grades, with vendors offering small handfuls to taste as you pass by.

CHICKEN AND PISTACHIO SOUP

METHOD

Put the whole chicken, carrot, celery, bay leaf and half of the onion in a saucepan. Add just enough cold water to cover and bring to a gentle simmer. Cook over low heat for 45 minutes, or until the chicken is tender; do not allow the liquid to simmer hard or the chicken will be tough. Remove the chicken and cool. Strain and reserve the cooking liquid, discarding the vegetables — you should have 6 cups stock; add extra water if necessary. Remove the chicken meat, discarding the skin, fat and bones. Finely shred the chicken and set aside.

Melt the butter in a saucepan over medium-low heat, then add the remaining onion and cook for 8 minutes, or until softened. Add the flour and cook for 3 minutes, stirring to combine. Add 1 cup of the reserved cooking liquid and stir constantly until the mixture has boiled and thickened. Continue adding the stock, 1 cup at a time, and stirring constantly between additions, until all the stock is used and the soup is quite thick.

Place the pistachios into a food processor and process until very finely ground. Add the milk, cream, chicken meat and pistachios to the soup and heat gently until just simmering; do not allow the soup to boil or it will curdle; season with salt and pepper.

Divide the soup among bowls and sprinkle with the extra chopped pistachios, to serve. **SERVES 4-6**

INGREDIENTS

2 lb 4 oz whole chicken
1 carrot, chopped
1 celery stick, chopped
1 bay leaf
2 onions, chopped
¼ cup butter
⅓ cup all-purpose flour
¾ cup shelled unsalted pistachios,
     plus extra, chopped, to serve
½ cup whole milk
½ cup whipping cream
sea salt
freshly ground black pepper

CELERIAC, SAFFRON AND MUSSEL SOUP

METHOD

Sprinkle the saffron threads into a small bowl with $\frac{1}{3}$ cup hot water and set aside for 1 hour, or until the liquid is a deep yellow color.

Put the stock in a large saucepan and bring to a boil. Add half of the mussels, cover the pan, and cook over high heat for about 3 minutes, or until the mussels have opened. Remove to a bowl using a slotted spoon and repeat with the remaining mussels until all are cooked. Discard any mussels that do not open. Reserve the cooking liquid. Remove the meat, discarding the shells, and reserve any juices in a bowl.

Meanwhile, heat the olive oil in a large saucepan over medium heat. Add the onion, garlic and celery and cook for 5–6 minutes, stirring often, until softened. Add the celeriac, potato and bay leaf, stirring to combine well, then cover and cook for 10–12 minutes, or until the vegetables have softened. Add the reserved stock, any mussel juices and the saffron mixture, and bring the soup to a simmer. Cook, uncovered, over medium-low heat for 8–10 minutes. Add the shelled mussels to the pan, season with salt and pepper, and continue cooking for about 2 minutes, or until the mussels are just heated through. Stir in the parsley and serve immediately. **SERVES 4–6**

INGREDIENTS

$\frac{1}{2}$ teaspoon saffron threads

4 cups fish or chicken stock

4 lb 8 oz black mussels, beards
    removed and shells scrubbed

$2\frac{1}{2}$ tablespoons extra virgin olive oil

2 onions, chopped

3 garlic cloves, finely chopped

3 celery sticks, cut into $\frac{1}{4}$-inch pieces

1 lb 9 oz celeriac, trimmed, peeled
    and cut into $\frac{1}{4}$-inch-thick slices

14 oz all-purpose potatoes, cut into
    $\frac{1}{2}$-inch pieces

1 fresh bay leaf

sea salt

freshly ground black pepper

$\frac{1}{2}$ cup Italian parsley leaves,
    coarsely chopped

TANDOOR BREAD AND WILD HERBS IN A KURDISH VILLAGE

I hire an English-speaking driver to take me somewhere — anywhere — where I can observe everyday village life. His choice is a village near the small town of Gevaş, about sixty kilometers south of Van. It turns out to be tiny, Kurdish, and has a dreamy setting among huge old trees at the base of steep hills. A small stream bubbles past the squat sand-colored stone houses and the whole place is a hub of activity. Food activity!

First I'm taken into a dark, smoke-filled room where women are hard at work around a tandoor oven — a cylindrical clay oven set into a hole in the ground (in Turkish its name is *gömme tandir*, meaning "buried tandoor") and fired by wood. Unlike more Westernized parts of Turkey, here the tandoor is a necessity — most of the old homes don't have their own ovens and households share in the preparation of items such as bread. I watch as one woman scoops up handfuls of sloppy dough from a large tub and shapes them into perfect, round balls. Another deftly rolls the dough into thin disks. These are then moistened slightly and slapped against the side of the tandoor with the aid of a round, padded block. They stick perfectly and are retrieved five minutes later, crisp, golden and steaming. It's repetitive, back-breaking work as they make dozens of loaves at a time, enough to feed several families for a week.

Outside, a young girl is washing chive-like herbs that emit a strong, garlic-like fragrance. This is the herb *sarmisakotu*, used to flavor the famous *otlu peynir* or "grassy cheese" for which Van is famous. The manufacture of *otlu peynir* is a highly seasonal endeavor. The herbs are picked in spring from the hills surrounding Van, where they grow wild, and the milk (mainly from sheep) is most plentiful then, too. Throughout June the villagers make cheese for their own consumption — it is brined then aged in tubs in the ground for about six months, where it becomes progressively more pungent, crumbly and salty. In July and August they make more cheese, but this is to sell.

Before we leave we dine on *ayran asi*, the yogurt-based soup that's enjoyed throughout the Kurdish southeast. It's served warm and is thick with chickpeas, soft boiled wheat, spinach and herbs. It's tasty, nourishing food served with chunks of the tandoor bread we watched being made earlier. We're sent home with a floppy round of bread each, wrapped in newspaper and still faintly warm and smoky from the oven.

RED LENTIL SOUP WITH MINTED EGGPLANT

METHOD

Heat 2 tablespoons of the olive oil in a large saucepan over medium heat. Add the onion and cook for 6–7 minutes, or until softened. Add the lentils and stock, then bring to a simmer, skimming the surface to remove any impurities. Reduce the heat to low, partially cover the pan, and simmer for 40–50 minutes, or until the lentils are very soft and have collapsed. Add the lemon juice and season with salt and pepper.

Meanwhile, sprinkle 2 tablespoons salt over the chopped eggplant in a colander and set aside for 20 minutes. Rinse the eggplant well, then drain and pat dry with paper towels. Heat the remaining olive oil in a large, heavy-based frying pan over medium-high heat. Add the eggplant and cook for 5–6 minutes, turning often, until golden and tender. Add the garlic and cook for 2 minutes, then add the mint and paprika and cook for another 2 minutes, or until fragrant.

To serve, divide the soup among bowls, spoon over the eggplant and garlic mixture, and scatter with the mint. **SERVES 6**

INGREDIENTS

$2/3$ cup extra virgin olive oil

2 onions, finely chopped

$2\frac{1}{2}$ cups red lentils

$2\frac{3}{4}$ quarts chicken or vegetable stock

$\frac{1}{4}$ cup freshly squeezed lemon
     juice, or to taste

sea salt

freshly ground black pepper

1 large eggplant cut into $\frac{1}{2}$-inch pieces

2 garlic cloves, crushed

3 teaspoons dried mint

$2\frac{1}{2}$ teaspoons sweet paprika

3 tablespoons chopped fresh mint, to serve

BREAD, PASTRY AND PASTA

Bread plays such a significant role in Turkey that it is traditionally regarded as sacred and wasting the leftovers, a sin. No Turkish meal is complete without bread, typically baked to golden crustiness in wood-fired ovens. Both leavened and unleavened breads feature in Turkish baking, as do myriad pastries, particularly börek, the making of which is considered something of an art form. Yufka dough, a traditional dough, somewhat thicker than filo pastry, forms the basis of many Turkish pastries and takes skill and patience to perfect — ideally it is rolled out using a long, thin rolling pin called an *olava*.

LAHMACUN

DOUGH

1 pinch sugar

2 teaspoons dried yeast

4 cups all-purpose flour, plus extra,
  for dusting

2 teaspoons sea salt

1 red onion, finely chopped

2 garlic cloves, finely chopped

1 lb 5 oz ground lamb

$1\frac{1}{2}$ tablespoons Turkish pepper paste
  (see note page 13)

sea salt

freshly ground black pepper

2 ripe tomatoes, quartered, seeded
  and chopped

1 red bell pepper, seeded, ribs
  removed and finely chopped

1 handful Italian parsley,
  leaves chopped

1 handful cilantro leaves, chopped

$\frac{1}{2}$ teaspoon dried chili flakes, plus extra
  to serve

lemon wedges, to serve

DOUGH

Combine the sugar and $\frac{1}{2}$ cup lukewarm water in a small bowl, then sprinkle over the yeast. Set aside for about 8 minutes, or until foamy, then add another $1\frac{1}{2}$ cups lukewarm water.

Combine the flour and salt in a bowl, then add the yeast mixture and stir to form a coarse dough. Turn out onto a lightly floured surface and knead for 5 minutes, or until the dough is smooth and elastic. Roll the dough into a ball and place in a lightly oiled bowl, turning to coat. Cover with plastic wrap and set aside in a warm, draft-free place for 1 hour, or until doubled in size.

Meanwhile, combine the onion, garlic, lamb and pepper paste in a bowl and season with salt and pepper. Using your hands, knead together for 5 minutes, or until very well combined — the mixture should be smooth and sticky. Add the tomato, bell pepper, parsley, cilantro and chili flakes, and gently knead until well combined.

Preheat the oven to 425°F. Line two baking sheets with parchment paper. Punch the dough down and turn out onto a lightly floured work surface and divide it into 12 even-sized balls. Roll each ball into a 10-x-$5\frac{1}{2}$-inch oval using a rolling pin. Spread each oval thinly with some of the lamb mixture, leaving a $\frac{1}{2}$-inch border around the edge.

Gently transfer the lahmacun to the prepared trays and bake, in batches, for 10–15 minutes, or until the dough is golden and crisp. Serve hot with the lemon wedges and extra chili flakes on the side. **MAKES 12**

SWEET TAHINI SPIRALS

METHOD

Combine the sugar and $\frac{1}{2}$ cup lukewarm water in a small bowl, then sprinkle over the yeast. Set aside for about 8 minutes, or until foamy. Combine the lukewarm milk and the beaten eggs, then add to the yeast mixture with another 2 tablespoons lukewarm water and the olive oil, stirring well to combine.

Combine the flour and salt in a bowl, then add the yeast mixture and stir to form a coarse dough. Turn out onto a lightly floured surface and knead for 5 minutes, or until the dough is smooth and elastic. Roll the dough into a ball and place in a lightly oiled bowl, turning to coat. Cover with plastic wrap and set aside in a warm, draft-free place for 1 hour, or until doubled in size.

Meanwhile, put the tahini, superfine sugar and the whole egg in a bowl, mixing until well combined — the mixture will become quite thick.

Punch the dough down and turn out onto a lightly floured work surface and divide it into 12 even-sized balls. Working with one ball at a time, roll each out into a circle with a 7-inch diameter using a rolling pin. Spread 1 tablespoon of the tahini mixture on each round, leaving a $\frac{1}{2}$-inch border around the edge. Roll up each to form a long sausage shape and continue to roll until it's about 12 inches long. Use your hands to shape each sausage into a tight spiral — each spiral should be about 4 inches in diameter — then flatten slightly. Transfer to lightly greased baking sheets, cover loosely with a dish towel, and set aside for about 30 minutes, or until puffy.

Preheat the oven to 425°F. Brush the top of each spiral with the egg yolk mixture and sprinkle lightly with sesame seeds. Bake for 30 minutes, or until golden and cooked through. Transfer to a wire rack to cool. Tahini spirals are best eaten on the day of making but will keep, frozen in an airtight container, for up to 1 month. **MAKES 12**

INGREDIENTS

1 large pinch sugar

3 teaspoons dried yeast

$\frac{2}{3}$ cup lukewarm milk

3 eggs; 2 lightly beaten, plus 1 egg yolk
 whisked with $1\frac{1}{2}$ tablespoons water

$2\frac{1}{2}$ tablespoons extra virgin olive oil

4 cups all-purpose flour

2 teaspoons sea salt

1 cup tahini

1 cup superfine sugar

sesame seeds, for sprinkling

LAMB, LENTIL AND MINT FILO PIES

INGREDIENTS

$\frac{3}{4}$ cup brown lentils

2 tablespoons olive oil

1 large onion, finely chopped

2 garlic cloves, finely chopped

14 oz ground lamb

2 tablespoons Turkish pepper paste
(see note page 13)

2 teaspoons sweet paprika

$\frac{1}{4}$ cup chopped mint

$\frac{1}{4}$ cup chopped Italian parsley

$\frac{1}{2}$ cup crumbled goat's cheese
(optional)

18 sheets filo pastry

$\frac{1}{2}$ cup butter, melted

Greek yogurt, to serve

METHOD

Put the lentils in a saucepan and add enough cold water to just cover. Bring to a simmer over medium-low heat and cook for 35–40 minutes, or until tender. Drain well.

Meanwhile, heat the olive oil in a large, heavy-based frying pan over medium heat. Add the onion and garlic and cook for 5–6 minutes, or until softened. Add the lamb and cook for 12–15 minutes, stirring often to break up the meat, until the lamb is browned and all excess liquid has evaporated — the meat should be quite dry. Add the pepper paste and paprika and cook for 2 minutes, stirring well. Remove from the heat and stir in the mint, parsley and goat's cheese, if using. Cool to room temperature.

Preheat the oven to 350°F and line a baking sheet with parchment paper. Lay the filo sheets on a clean work surface and cover with a damp dish towel to prevent them from drying out while you work. Take one sheet of filo pastry and place it with the long edge closest to you. Brush all over with melted butter, then place another sheet of pastry on top. Brush with melted butter, then place another sheet of pastry over it. Brush the top layer with butter and spoon a thin line of the lamb mixture in a strip down the long side of pastry nearest you, leaving a $\frac{3}{4}$-inch border at each short end. Roll up lengthwise to form a skinny log, then shape the log into a tight spiral.

Transfer each spiral to the prepared sheets and repeat with the remaining pastry and filling to make six spirals total. Brush the remaining melted butter over the top of each spiral and bake in the oven for 35 minutes, or until deep golden. Serve hot with yogurt on the side. **MAKES 6**

The Turks have many flat breads in their repertoire, both leavened and unleavened. This one is inspired by *sac ekmeği* (a sac is a large convex griddle that originated in early nomadic life when cooking apparatus had to be portable). A large heavy-based, cast-iron frying pan works well in the absence of a sac.

FLAT BREAD

METHOD

Combine the sugar and $\frac{1}{2}$ cup lukewarm water in a small bowl and sprinkle over the yeast. Set aside for about 8 minutes, or until foamy, then add $\frac{1}{4}$ cup lukewarm water.

Combine the flour and salt in a bowl, then add the yeast mixture and stir to form a coarse dough. Turn out onto a lightly floured surface and knead for 5 minutes, or until the dough is smooth and elastic. Roll the dough into a ball and place in a lightly oiled bowl, turning to coat. Cover with plastic wrap and set aside in a warm, draft-free place for 1 hour, or until doubled in size.

Punch the dough down and turn out onto a lightly floured work surface and divide it into 12 even-sized balls. Roll each ball into a circle with a $9\frac{1}{2}$-inch diameter, using a rolling pin. Heat a large non-stick frying pan over medium heat and cook the flat breads, one at a time, for 3 minutes on each side, or until cooked through and just colored. Remove to a plate to keep warm while you cook the remaining flat breads. Serve warm or at room temperature. Flat breads are best served on the day of making but will keep, frozen in an airtight plastic bag, for up to 4 weeks. **MAKES 12**

INGREDIENTS

1 teaspoon superfine sugar

$1\frac{1}{2}$ teaspoons dried yeast

4 cups all-purpose flour

$1\frac{1}{2}$ teaspoons sea salt

SWISS CHARD, FETA AND GOLDEN RAISIN PIDE

SWISS CHARD, FETA AND SULTANA FILLING

Finely chop the Swiss chard stems and coarsely chop the leaves. Heat the olive oil in a large saucepan over medium heat. Add the onion and garlic and cook for 5 minutes, or until softened. Add the golden raisin and chard stems, cover the pan, and cook for 10 minutes, stirring occasionally, until the stems are soft. Coarsely chop the spinach stems and leaves, then add to the pan with the chard leaves, cover, and cook for 3 minutes, or until the spinach has wilted. Season with salt and pepper, then remove from the heat and cool slightly. Stir in the feta.

Preheat the oven to 400°F and lightly grease two large baking sheets. Punch the dough down and turn out onto a lightly floured work surface and divide the dough into eight even-sized pieces. Working with one piece of dough at a time, roll each piece into a 10-x-6¼-inch oval, using a rolling pin. Place one-sixth of the filling in the middle of each oval, leaving a 1-inch border around the edge, then pull the dough up around the edges to partially cover the filling, pleating the edge. Transfer to the prepared sheets, brush the top and side with the egg yolk mixture and bake, in batches, for 15–20 minutes, or until the dough is deep golden and the filling is bubbling. Serve hot or warm. **MAKES 8**

Variation: To make the beef and kashkaval filling, cut the steak into ½-inch pieces and set aside. Heat half of the olive oil in a large frying pan over medium-high heat. Add the meat and cook for 5 minutes, stirring often, until browned. Remove from the heat and set aside.

Heat the remaining oil in a saucepan over medium heat. Add the onion and garlic and cook for 5–6 minutes, stirring often, until softened. Add the pepper paste, tomato paste, paprika, oregano and chili flakes (if using) and cook for 1–2 minutes, or until fragrant. Add the meat, tomato and ¼ cup water. Bring to a simmer and cook over low heat for 50 minutes, or until the meat is very tender and the liquid has reduced. Season with salt and pepper, then remove from the heat and cool to room temperature.

Roll and shape the pide as directed, but use the cheese as the filling and spoon the meat over the top once you have pleated the dough. Brush with the egg yolk mixture and bake, in batches, for 15–20 minutes, or until the dough is deep golden. **MAKES 8**

SWISS CHARD, FETA AND SULTANA FILLING

1 lb 5 oz Swiss chard, 2½ inches trimmed from stems

2½ tablespoons extra virgin olive oil

1 large onion, finely chopped

3 garlic cloves, finely chopped

½ cup golden raisins

1 lb 5 oz spinach, 1¼ inches trimmed from stems

sea salt

freshly ground black pepper

1⅓ cups crumbled feta cheese

1 portion Pide dough (see page 85)

1 egg yolk beaten with 1½ tablespoons water

(VARIATION) BEEF AND KASHKAVAL FILLING

2 lb 4 oz chuck steak

⅓ cup olive oil

1 large onion, chopped

2 garlic cloves, crushed

1½ tablespoons Turkish pepper paste (see note page 13)

1 tablespoon tomato paste

2 teaspoons paprika

2½ tablespoons oregano leaves

1 teaspoon dried chili flakes (optional)

14 oz can chopped tomatoes

sea salt

freshly ground black pepper

2 cups grated kashkaval cheese (see note page 74)

1 egg yolk beaten with 1½ tablespoons water

CHEESE AND POTATO FILO ROLLS

INGREDIENTS

1 lb 7 oz all-purpose potatoes,
    peeled and quartered

2 tablespoons extra virgin olive oil

1 onion, finely chopped

1 garlic clove, crushed

$1\frac{1}{3}$ cups crumbled feta cheese

$\frac{1}{2}$ teaspoon ground allspice

$2\frac{1}{2}$ tablespoons chopped mint

$2\frac{1}{2}$ tablespoons chopped Italian parsley

1 egg, lightly beaten

sea salt

freshly ground black pepper

14 sheets filo pastry

$\frac{3}{4}$ cup butter, melted

nigella seeds or sesame seeds,
    for sprinkling

METHOD

Cook the potato in salted boiling water for 15 minutes or until tender. Drain well and cool slightly. Heat the olive oil in a large saucepan over medium heat. Add the onion and garlic, and cook for 6–7 minutes, or until softened. Remove from the heat, add the potato and use a potato masher to mash into a coarse purée. Stir in the feta, allspice, mint, parsley and egg until well combined. Season with salt and pepper.

Preheat the oven to 350°F and lightly grease a large baking sheet. Lay the filo sheets on a clean work surface and cover with a damp dish towel to prevent them from drying out while you work. Take one sheet of filo pastry and brush with melted butter, then lay another sheet over the top and brush lightly with butter. Cut the pastry into four even quarters. Working with one piece at a time, take 1 tablespoonful of the potato mixture and form into a neat log about $3\frac{1}{4}$ inches long. Place a log along the long edge of each pastry quarter, then roll up, folding in the ends as you roll, taking care not to roll too tightly or the pastry could burst while baking. Place the pastry rolls onto the prepared sheets, seam-side down. Repeat with the remaining filo and filling — you should make 28 rolls in total. Brush the tops of the rolls with the remaining melted butter and sprinkle generously with nigella seeds.

Bake in the oven for 20–30 minutes, or until light golden. Serve warm.
MAKES 28

URFA: WOOD-FIRED BREAD AND FAMOUS PEPPERS

When in public you could be forgiven for thinking that Turkey beats to a distinctly male-oriented drum, and nowhere is this played out more clearly than in the many wood-fired bakeries scattered around the city of Urfa. These bakeries are a hub of activity, with their deep stone ovens and inviting aromas of freshly baked bread. Typically, a group of men stand in a line vigorously kneading, shaping and rolling dough into flat loaves, while others, sweaty from their exertions, work the inferno, removing baked loaves and depositing uncooked ones into the hot glowing coals using long wooden paddles. On any given morning customers, all male, drop by the bakeries with armfuls of eggplants and shiny red bell peppers, which they deposit, along with their bread orders. They then return ten minutes later to pick up their steaming loaves and the vegetables, which have since been charred to crunchy perfection. This is breakfast in Urfa!

At lunch time I stand outside another *firin*, or communal oven, and watch as men and boys dash in with trays of food (typically a simple layered arrangement of meat and seasonal vegetables) before rushing off to midday prayers. About forty minutes later, they swing past to pick up the bread with their hot lunch. It's clearly a daily ritual, and one from which the women seem largely absent; when I do see women out and about they tend to be in the company of a male relative or another woman at least. Certainly not alone.

But there is another incentive for visiting this seductive city. All over Turkey, wherever you dine, food is offered with little paots or shakers of hot dried chili flakes — the most celebrated of these come from Kahramanaras (also famed for its stretchy ice cream, known as dondurma) and from Urfa. The Urfa pepper is, in its most desirable form, an artisanal product. The peppers grow in the barren countryside around the city and, because they ripen at different rates, are all picked by hand. Many producers still dry them the ancient way, in the sun, then ferment them slightly afterwards. This gives the processed flakes their characteristic ox-blood color and unmistakable flavor of earth and smoke. The taste is addictive and the sight and smell of them in the bazaars, heaped in great cones awaiting sale, is tantalizing. And wholly unforgettable.

Simit is, for me, the quintessential Turkish food. To describe these round, chewy bread rings as "sesame-encrusted bread" really isn't doing them justice; their flavor and deeply satisfying texture are quite unlike anything else. Turks eat simit daily, as a snack, but they really come into their own as fortifying breakfast fare, accompanied by cheese, tomatoes, cucumbers and olives.

SIMIT

METHOD

Combine the sugar and $\frac{1}{4}$ cup lukewarm water in a small bowl, then sprinkle over the yeast. Set aside for about 8 minutes, or until foamy, then add another $1\frac{1}{4}$ cups lukewarm water.

Combine the flour and salt in a bowl, then add the yeast mixture and stir to form a coarse dough. Turn out onto a lightly floured surface and knead for 6–7 minutes, or until the dough is smooth and elastic. Roll the dough into a ball and place in a lightly oiled bowl, turning to coat. Cover with plastic wrap and set aside in a warm, draft-free place for 1 hour, or until doubled in size.

Preheat the oven to 425°F and line two baking sheets with parchment paper. Punch the dough down and turn out onto a lightly floured work surface and divide it into 10 even-sized pieces. Combine the pekmez with $\frac{1}{3}$ cup water in a large bowl. Place the sesame seeds on a large plate. Working with one piece of dough at a time, use your hands to roll the dough out to make ten 22-inch-long ropes. Fold in half so the two ends align, then lift off the board and use your hands to twist each rectangle into a two-stranded "rope." Place back on the work surface and join the ends together to make a circle, pressing the ends firmly together to seal. Repeat with the remaining dough to make 10 rope circles.

Dip each ring, first into the pekmez mixture, immersing completely to coat, then drain well and toss in the sesame seeds, turning gently to coat. Transfer to the prepared sheets and set aside at room temperature for about 20 minutes, to puff slightly. Bake in the oven for 15–18 minutes, or until deep golden and cooked through. Transfer to a wire rack to cool. Simit are best eaten on the day of making but will keep, frozen in an airtight container, for up to 1 month. **MAKES 10**

Note: Pekmez is a molasses-like syrup made from the juice and must of certain fruits, usually grapes or figs. It is available from Middle Eastern and Turkish grocery stores.

INGREDIENTS

1 pinch sugar

3 teaspoons dried yeast

$3\frac{1}{3}$ cups all-purpose flour

$1\frac{1}{2}$ teaspoons sea salt

$\frac{2}{3}$ cup pekmez (see note)

$1\frac{1}{2}$ cups sesame seeds

LEEK AND FAVA BEAN BÖREK

DOUGH

$2\,^2/_3$ cups all-purpose flour

2 eggs, lightly beaten

2 tablespoons olive oil

1 tablespoon white vinegar

$^1/_3$ cup Greek yogurt

1 teaspoon sea salt

5 tablespoons butter, plus extra for greasing

3 lb leeks, trimmed, rinsed and
      finely sliced

$2\,^1/_4$ lb fava beans, podded

7 oz grated kashkaval cheese (see note)

$^1/_2$ teaspoon freshly grated nutmeg

3 eggs

sea salt

freshly ground black pepper

$^2/_3$ cup whole milk

DOUGH

Place the flour in a bowl and make a well in the center. In a separate bowl, combine the remaining ingredients with $^1/_4$ cup water and whisk well to combine. Add to the flour, and gently combine to form a soft dough, adding an extra 1 tablespoon water if the dough is too stiff. Turn out onto a lightly floured work surface and knead for 3 minutes, or until smooth and elastic. Place in a lightly oiled bowl, cover with plastic wrap and stand at cool room temperature for 30 minutes.

Meanwhile, heat half the butter in a large saucepan over medium heat. Add the leeks, cover, then reduce the heat to medium-low and cook for 25 minutes, stirring often until leeks are very soft. Drain in a colander and cool.

Cook the fava beans in salted boiling water for 5–6 minutes, drain well, then cool under running water. Drain again and peel and discard the tough outer skins. Combine the leek and cheese in a bowl. Lightly beat two of the eggs and add to the leek mixture. Stir in the fava beans and season with salt and pepper.

Melt the remaining butter and add to a separate bowl with the milk and remaining egg, stirring well to combine.

Grease the base and sides of two 8-inch round cake pans with butter. Divide the dough into eight even-sized portions. Roll each portion out on a lightly floured work surface to make a circle, about $^1/_{16}$ inch thick, taking care the pastry does not tear. Line each pan with a pastry round, carefully easing it into the corners and allowing the excess to overhang. Brush the milk mixture generously over the pastry and add another layer of pastry to each pan. Brush with milk again and add another layer of pastry over the top — you should have three layers of pastry for each pie base. Divide the filling between both bases.

Cut both of the remaining dough portions in half again. Roll each half out into thin circles with an 8-inch diameter for the lids. Place over each pie and brush with the milk mixture. Place the remaining pastry over the top, creating two layers of pastry for each lid, and brush with the milk mixture. Bring any overhanging pastry up from the side, stretching it if necessary to pull it at least part-way over the top. Bake for 1 hour, or until the pastry is golden and cooked through. Serve warm or at room temperature. **SERVES 10-12**

Note: Kashkaval cheese is a semihard cheese that is popular throughout the Balkans as well as Turkey, where it is often made from sheep's milk.

BEET GREEN, RICOTTA AND HAZELNUT GÖZLEME

METHOD

Combine the flour and salt in a large bowl and make a well in the center. Add 1 cup water and 2 tablespoons of the olive oil and stir with a flat-bladed knife, gradually incorporating more of the flour into the liquid as you go, until a coarse, soft dough forms. Turn out onto a lightly floured surface and knead for 5–6 minutes, or until smooth and elastic, adding a little extra flour if the dough is too sticky. (Take care not to add too much flour as the dough should be soft.) Roll the dough into a ball and place in a lightly oiled bowl, turning to coat. Cover with plastic wrap and set aside in a warm, draft-free place for 1 hour.

Meanwhile, heat the remaining oil in a saucepan over medium heat. Add the garlic and cook for 2 minutes, or until fragrant. Add the raisins and beet greens and stalks, cover the pan, and cook for 6 minutes, or until softened. Increase the heat to high, add the spinach and cook for 2–3 minutes, or until the spinach has wilted. Remove the greens mixture to a bowl using a slotted spoon, then continue to boil the pan juices for 3–4 minutes, or until reduced to about 2 tablespoons. Add to the greens mixture in the bowl and cool to room temperature. Add the nutmeg, ricotta and hazelnuts, season with sea salt and pepper, then gently stir to just combine.

Line two baking sheets with parchment paper. Divide the dough into 12 even-sized pieces. Working with one piece of dough at a time, roll each into a ball using your hands. Use a rolling pin to then roll into circles, each with an $8\frac{1}{4}$-inch diameter. Place 2 tablespoons of the filling on one side of each circle. Brush the edge of each circle lightly with the egg. Fold the dough over to make half-moon shapes and pinch to seal and enclose the filling. Place on the prepared baking sheets, press down to flatten slightly, and sprinkle with extra flour.

Heat about 1 tablespoon of oil in a large, heavy-based frying pan over medium heat and cook the gözleme, in batches, for 4–5 minutes on each side, or until deep golden and the filling is heated through. Serve immediately.
MAKES 12

INGREDIENTS

2 cups all-purpose flour, plus extra
    for dusting

1 teaspoon salt

$\frac{1}{3}$ cup olive oil, plus extra for cooking

3 garlic cloves, thinly sliced

$\frac{1}{2}$ cup golden raisins

leaves and stalks from 2 bunches beets,
    rinsed and chopped

12 oz spinach, rinsed and chopped

1 large pinch freshly grated nutmeg

1 cup crumbled ricotta salata cheese

$\frac{3}{4}$ cup hazelnuts, roasted, skinned
    and chopped

sea salt

freshly ground black pepper

1 egg, lightly beaten

CAPPADOCIA AND A WISTFUL DREAM OF YUFKA DOUGH

Situated in the heart of Anatolia, the region of Cappadocia is famed worldwide for its singular landscapes and quirky vernacular architecture. The amazing "fairy chimney" rock dwellings, hewn from cliff faces and rising dramatically out of the volcanic tuff, is part of the reason the area has such enormous historical significance. It has been settled for millennia, notably by the Hittites as far back as 2000 BC, and has an eerie atmosphere, unique to well-worn places that have seen humans come and go for a very long time. Persecuted early Christians took refuge in deep valleys, carving homes, churches and monasteries out of entire hills and high into rock walls. They left behind a veritable trove of Byzantine art, troglodyte villages and underground towns.

I stay in a guesthouse in Göreme, an admittedly pretty town, but one that has given over to tourism in such a way that it has arguably lost its soul. The guesthouse owner is an anthropologist who first visited from his native Germany some thirty years ago to study Cappadocian dwellings. In the relatively few decades since then, he's witnessed the complete disintegration of traditional life in the town and I find the subject fascinating. Back in the 1980s, he saw how local women would gather annually, several households together, to make enough sheets of yufka dough to last them through the year. They'd bury themselves deep in mixing, kneading and rolling the dough for days on end until the job was done. It was real secret women's business, he tells me. "They didn't just make yufka — it was an important time for bonding, sorting out problems and differences, venting about husbands and imparting advice to the younger ones. It was part of what held the community together."

Once made, the fragile yufka dough would keep in the dry, cool interiors of the traditional rock homes without spoiling, almost indefinitely. Today, this activity, like many other traditional, communal practices, has gone the way of the fez. People run internet cafés and bars for backpackers or get up early to bundle visitors into crammed hot-air balloon baskets — the "essential" Cappadocian experience. They buy their yufka from the market. Despite this realization I can't help but start fantasizing about how the baked yufka dough, rolled into thin circular sheets and baked on hot iron plates, would taste. My mind runs riot with the many possible uses I could find for it.

78   TURKEY

HOMEMADE PASTA WITH ARUGULA, FETA, WALNUTS AND HERBS

ERISTE PASTA

Whisk the eggs and milk in a bowl until well combined. Sift the flour and sea salt into a large bowl, stir in the semolina and make a well in the center. Add the egg and milk mixture and stir with a fork to form a soft dough. Turn out onto a lightly floured surface and knead for 5 minutes, or until the dough is smooth and elastic. Roll the dough into a ball and place in a lightly oiled bowl, turning to coat. Cover with plastic wrap and set aside.

Turn the dough out onto a lightly floured surface and divide into two even-sized pieces. Working with one piece at a time, roll into a 24-x-16-inch rectangle, using a rolling pin. Cut each rectangle into thirds lengthwise. Arrange the pasta sheets between layers of lightly floured dish towels and set aside at room temperature for 8 hours to dry slightly. Transfer to a board and cut each strip lengthwise into $\frac{1}{2}$-inch-wide strips and dust lightly with flour.

Bring a large saucepan of salted water to a boil. Add the pasta and cook for 5–6 minutes, or until *al dente*. Drain well and set aside, reserving about $\frac{1}{2}$ cup of the cooking water.

Meanwhile, heat the olive oil in a large, deep frying pan or saucepan over medium heat. Add the garlic and walnuts and cook for 3 minutes, or until the garlic is fragrant. Add the arugula, parsley and dill and stir for 1–2 minutes, or until wilted. Add the cooked pasta and enough of the reserved cooking liquid to moisten the pasta. Add the feta and toss gently to combine. Divide the pasta among serving plates and serve immediately. **SERVES 4**

ERISTE PASTA

2 eggs, lightly beaten

7 fl oz whole milk

2$\frac{2}{3}$ cups all-purpose
    flour, plus extra for dusting

1$\frac{1}{2}$ teaspoons sea salt

$\frac{1}{2}$ cup fine semolina

$\frac{1}{2}$ cup extra virgin olive oil

3 garlic cloves, finely chopped

1 cup chopped walnuts

1 bunch arugula, rinsed and
    coarsely chopped

1 bunch Italian parsley, chopped

1 bunch fresh dill, chopped

1$\frac{1}{3}$ cups crumbled feta cheese

DILL, LEMON AND FETA POĞAÇA

INGREDIENTS

1 cup whole milk

5 tablespoons butter

$\frac{1}{4}$ cup superfine sugar

3 teaspoons dried yeast

1 egg, lightly beaten

$\frac{1}{4}$ cup chopped fresh dill

finely grated zest of 2 lemons

$4\frac{1}{2}$ cups all-purpose flour

$2\frac{1}{2}$ teaspoons sea salt

7 oz feta cheese, cubed

METHOD

Put the milk and butter in a small saucepan over low heat until the mixture is lukewarm. Remove from the heat and set aside.

Combine the sugar and $\frac{1}{2}$ cup lukewarm water in a small bowl, then sprinkle over the yeast. Set aside for about 8 minutes, or until foamy.

Combine the yeast and milk mixtures in a large bowl and add the egg, dill and lemon zest, stirring well to combine. Add 4 cups of the flour and the salt, and stir to form a coarse dough. Add a little of the remaining flour if the dough is too wet — it should still be a little soft so take care not to add too much flour. Turn out onto a lightly floured surface and knead for 5–6 minutes, or until the dough is smooth and elastic. Roll the dough into a ball and place in a lightly oiled bowl, turning to coat. Cover with plastic wrap and set aside in a warm, draft-free place for 1 hour, or until doubled in size.

Preheat the oven to 350°F and lightly grease two baking sheets. Punch the dough down and turn out onto a lightly floured surface and divide into 12 even-sized pieces. Use your hands to roll each piece into a ball. Flatten each ball into a disk and divide the cubed feta among the rounds. Bring the edges of each disk together to form balls again and enclose the feta, then roll over the work surface to neaten. Transfer to the prepared sheets and cover loosely with a damp dish towel, then set aside for 30 minutes or until risen slightly.

Bake in the oven for 20 minutes, or until golden and cooked through. Transfer to a wire rack to cool and serve at room temperature. Poğaça are best served on the day of making but will keep, frozen in an airtight container, for up to 1 month. **MAKES 12**

CHICKEN AND BLACK-EYED PEA MANTI

YUFKA DOUGH

Place the flour and salt in a large bowl and make a well in the center. Combine the egg in a bowl with $\frac{1}{2}$ cup water and whisk well to combine. Add to the flour and use your hands to mix together, adding a little more water as needed to form a soft dough. Turn out onto a lightly floured surface and knead for 3 minutes, or until smooth and elastic. Place in a lightly oiled bowl, cover with plastic wrap and refrigerate for 30 minutes.

Put the black-eyed peas in a saucepan and add just enough water to cover, then bring to a boil. Reduce the heat to low and simmer for 35 minutes, or until tender. Drain well, reserving 1 cup of the cooking liquid. Set aside.

Heat the 2 tablespoons of olive oil in a large saucepan over medium heat. Add the onion and garlic and cook for 5 minutes, or until softened. Add the tomato paste, allspice and half the paprika, and stir for 1–2 minutes, or until fragrant. Add the chicken, tomatoes, reserved cooking liquid and oregano. Bring to a simmer and cook over low heat for 50 minutes, or until the chicken is very tender. Remove the chicken and when cool enough to handle, remove the meat, discarding the skin and bones. Shred the meat coarsely.

Skim any excess fat from the tomato mixture, add the peas and simmer for 10–15 minutes, or until reduced and thickened slightly. Remove the oregano sprigs and return the chicken meat to the pan. Season with salt and pepper, then cover the pan and continue cooking for 5–10 minutes more, or until heated through.

Preheat the oven to 350°F and lightly grease a large baking sheet. Divide the dough into four even-sized pieces. Working with one piece of dough at a time, roll out on a lightly floured surface to a $14\frac{1}{4}$-x-$8\frac{1}{2}$-inch rectangle, using a rolling pin. Cut each rectangle in half widthwise, then cut strips, about $\frac{5}{8}$ inch wide. Place these strips on the prepared sheet and brush well with the melted butter. Bake in the oven, in batches, for 12–15 minutes, or until golden and crisp. When all the strips are baked, divide among shallow bowls, then spoon the chicken mixture over.

Heat the remaining butter until foaming, then add the remaining paprika and the chili flakes and drizzle the chicken sauce. Sprinkle with the parsley and serve with the yogurt passed separately. **SERVES 4**

YUFKA DOUGH

2 cups all-purpose flour

$\frac{1}{2}$ teaspoon sea salt

2 eggs, lightly beaten

$\frac{2}{3}$ cup black-eyed peas, soaked overnight and drained

2 tablespoons extra virgin olive oil, plus more for greasing

1 onion, finely chopped

4 garlic cloves, crushed

$2\frac{1}{2}$ tablespoons tomato paste

1 teaspoon ground allspice

1 tablespoon sweet paprika

10 oz chicken leg quarters

one 14 oz can chopped tomatoes

4 oregano sprigs

sea salt

freshly ground black pepper

5 tablespoons butter, melted, for brushing

1 teaspoon dried chili flakes, or to taste

1 cup Italian parsley leaves, chopped

Greek yogurt, to serve

Although we often tend to think of it as a type of pizza or Turkish flat bread, *pide* is actually the general name given to several types of bread loaves served throughout Turkey. They are baked in high-temperature ovens, often fired by wood, and are crusty and chewy. While the authentic effect is hard to emulate at home, this version is simple to make and tastes fantastic.

PIDE

METHOD

Heat the milk and butter in a small saucepan over low heat until the mixture is lukewarm. Remove from the heat and set aside.

Combine the sugar and $\frac{1}{2}$ cup lukewarm water in a small bowl, then sprinkle over the yeast. Set aside for about 8 minutes, or until foamy.

Combine the yeast and milk mixtures in a large bowl and add the flour and salt, stirring to form a coarse dough. Turn out onto a lightly floured surface and knead for 6–7 minutes, or until the dough is smooth and elastic. Roll the dough into a ball and place in a lightly oiled bowl, turning to coat. Cover with plastic wrap and set aside in a warm, draft-free place for 1 hour, or until doubled in size.

Preheat the oven to 400°F and lightly grease a large baking sheet. Punch the dough down and turn out onto a lightly floured work surface. Divide it into equal halves. Roll each half into a round with an $8\frac{1}{2}$-inch diameter, about $1\frac{1}{2}$ inches thick, using a rolling pin. Cover loosely with a dish towel and stand at room temperature for 30 minutes, or until risen slightly.

Brush each round with milk and use a very sharp knife to cut shallow $1\frac{1}{2}$-inch diamonds on top of the dough. Sprinkle with nigella seeds or sesame seeds, then bake for 30–35 minutes, or until golden and cooked through. Turn out onto a wire rack to cool. **MAKES 2 LOAVES**

INGREDIENTS

1 cup whole milk, plus extra for brushing

$\frac{1}{4}$ cup butter

$1\frac{1}{2}$ tablespoons superfine sugar

2 teaspoons dried yeast

$4\frac{1}{2}$ cups all-purpose flour

2 teaspoons sea salt

2 tablespoons nigella seeds or sesame seeds

Manti are the ravioli of Anatolia. They are admittedly a little fussy to make, as the dough needs to be rolled thinly and cut into fine squares, filled with a smidgeon of meat and sealed into neat little parcels. But the effort is well worth it — they taste delicious with yogurt and a slick of herb and spice butter.

CLASSIC MANTI

YUFKA DOUGH

2 cups all-purpose flour

1 teaspoon salt

2 eggs, lightly beaten

14 oz ground lamb or beef

1 small onion, finely chopped

1 garlic clove, crushed

sea salt

freshly ground black pepper

$\frac{1}{2}$ cup butter

2 teaspoons paprika

2 teaspoons dried mint

1 teaspoon dried chili flakes, or to taste

2 cups Greek yogurt

YUFKA DOUGH

Place the flour and salt in a large bowl and make a well in the center. Combine the egg in a bowl with $\frac{1}{2}$ cup water and whisk well to combine. Add to the flour and use your hands to mix together, adding a little more water as needed to form a soft dough. Turn out onto a lightly floured work surface and knead for 3 minutes, or until smooth and elastic. Place in a lightly oiled bowl, cover with plastic wrap and refrigerate for 30 minutes.

Combine the meat, onion and garlic in a bowl, season well with salt and pepper, then, using your hands, mix until well combined and smooth.

Divide the dough into four even-sized portions and cover with a damp dish towel to prevent them from drying out. Line two baking sheets with parchment paper. Working with one portion of dough at a time, roll out on a lightly floured surface to create a large, paper-thin rectangle; the dough should be extremely thin. (Lightly flour the rolling pin to ensure the dough does not tear.) Using a large, sharp knife, neaten the edges of the rectangle, then cut into $1\frac{1}{2}$-inch squares. Take $\frac{1}{2}$ teaspoon of the filling at a time and roll into tiny balls. Place a meatball in the middle of each square. Lift up the four corners to join in the middle, pressing to seal, and create a square parcel with seams running down each side. Place onto the prepared sheets and cover. Repeat this process with the remaining dough and filling until it is all used.

Bring a large saucepan of salted water to a boil and cook the manti, in batches, for 4–5 minutes each, or until they rise to the surface and the filling is cooked through. Drain well and divide among warm serving bowls.

Melt the butter in a frying pan over medium-high heat until it sizzles, then add the paprika, dried mint and chili flakes, and cook for 30 seconds or until the butter foams. Spoon the yogurt and drizzle the butter over the manti and serve immediately. **SERVES 4**

VEGETABLES AND SALADS

As a food-producing country, Turkey wants for nothing; it's one of the few nations in the world that grows more than it needs to feed itself. In Turkey, eating according to the seasons and buying locally is commonplace. A stroll through a Turkish produce market is a joy — in late summer the tomatoes and bell peppers are so ripe they're almost at bursting point, while in spring, artichokes, leeks and bunches of greens are fat and lush. The typical Turkish diet relies heavily on a variety of vegetables and these are prepared in such a way as to leave them tasting deeply and unforgettably of little but themselves.

PEKMEZ ROASTED PEAR, FETA, WATERCRESS AND HAZELNUT SALAD

METHOD

Preheat the oven to 350°F. Cut the unpeeled pears in half lengthwise and remove the cores. Cut the halves into thirds lengthwise, then place the pear wedges in a single layer in a small baking dish. Drizzle with the pekmez and olive oil and roast for about 30 minutes, turning once, until the pears are very tender and deep golden all over and the cooking juices are reduced and sticky. Remove from the oven and cool to room temperature.

DRESSING

Combine the vinegar, garlic, pekmez and cumin in a small bowl and whisk well to combine. Whisking constantly, slowly add the olive oil in a thin stream, then season with salt and pepper.

Spread the watercress over a serving platter, then scatter over the pear, cheese and hazelnuts. Drizzle the dressing over the top and serve. **SERVES 6**

INGREDIENTS

6 corella pears

$1\frac{1}{2}$ tablespoons pekmez (see note page 73)

1 tablespoon extra virgin olive oil

3 cups watercress

7 oz feta cheese or goat's cheese, crumbled

$\frac{1}{2}$ cup hazelnuts, roasted, peeled and chopped

DRESSING

2 tablespoons red wine vinegar

1 garlic clove, crushed

2 tablespoons pekmez

1 teaspoon cumin seeds, dry-roasted and crushed

$\frac{1}{2}$ cup extra virgin olive oil

sea salt

freshly ground black pepper

CRANBERRY BEAN PILAKI

INGREDIENTS

$1\frac{1}{2}$ cups dried cranberry beans,
    soaked overnight and drained

$\frac{1}{3}$ cup olive oil

2 onions, chopped

3 garlic cloves, finely chopped

1 carrot, finely chopped

1 red bell pepper, seeded, ribs
    removed and finely chopped

$2\frac{1}{2}$ teaspoons sweet paprika

$2\frac{1}{2}$ tablespoons Turkish pepper paste
    (see note page 13)

1 tablespoon superfine sugar

sea salt

freshly ground black pepper

1 handful Italian parsley,
    leaves chopped

extra virgin olive oil, to serve

METHOD

Put the cranberry beans in a saucepan and add just enough water to cover. Bring to a simmer and cook over medium heat for 30–40 minutes, or until just tender. Drain well.

Meanwhile, heat the olive oil in a large saucepan, add the onion, garlic, carrot and bell pepper and cook, stirring, for 15 minutes, or until the vegetables are tender. Add the paprika and pepper paste and cook, stirring well, for another 2 minutes, then add the drained beans, sugar and enough cold water to just cover the beans. Simmer over low heat, uncovered, for 1–$1\frac{1}{2}$ hours, or until the beans are tender and the liquid has reduced — the beans should not be soupy. Season with salt and pepper, then remove from the heat and cool to room temperature. Stir in the parsley, then serve drizzled with a little extra virgin olive oil. **SERVES 6**

LONG-COOKED BEANS AND OKRA

INGREDIENTS

$2\frac{1}{2}$ tablespoons olive oil

1 onion, finely chopped

2 garlic cloves, crushed

12 oz large green beans, trimmed

12 oz small okra, trimmed

2 teaspoons tomato paste

one 28-oz can chopped tomatoes

3 teaspoons sugar

sea salt

freshly ground black pepper

dill sprigs, to serve

METHOD

Heat the olive oil in a large saucepan over medium heat. Add the onion and garlic and cook for 5–7 minutes, or until softened. Add the beans, okra and tomato paste and cook, stirring, for 2 minutes. Add the tomato and sugar, bring to a simmer, then reduce the heat to low, cover the pan, and cook for 10 minutes. Remove the lid and simmer the beans for 20 minutes more, or until the liquid has reduced and the mixture has thickened. Remove from the heat and cool to room temperature. Season with salt and pepper and serve immediately with the dill as a garnish. **SERVES 6**

ZUCCHINI FRITTERS

METHOD

Place the grated zucchini in a colander, sprinkle with the salt, toss to combine well, then set aside for 20 minutes. Using your hands, squeeze the zucchini well to remove as much liquid as possible.

Heat 2 tablespoons of the olive oil in a large frying pan over medium heat. Add the onion and garlic and cook for 6–7 minutes, or until softened. Add the zucchini and cook, stirring, for another 4–5 minutes, or until the zucchini just starts to color. Remove from the heat, transfer to a large bowl and cool slightly. Add the flour, baking powder, egg, feta, parsley and dill and stir well to combine; season with salt and pepper.

Heat the remaining oil in a clean frying pan over medium heat, then cook mounded tablespoons of the zucchini mixture, in batches, for 3–4 minutes on each side, or until deep golden. Drain well on paper towels and serve immediately with the yogurt. **MAKES ABOUT 16**

Variation: You can make these fritters with carrots instead of zucchini if you prefer — simply substitute the zucchini with 1 lb 5 oz carrots. They need to be grated and squeezed dry in a clean dish towel before using. You can also add ¾ cup coarsely chopped dried apricots to the mix or use kashkaval cheese instead of feta. If you opt for this variation you can omit the dill.

INGREDIENTS

1 lb 10 oz zucchini, trimmed
    and coarsely grated
1½ teaspoons salt
½ cup extra virgin olive oil
1 large onion, finely chopped
2 garlic cloves, finely chopped
¾ cup all-purpose flour, sifted
1 teaspoon baking powder
3 eggs, lightly beaten
1½ cups crumbled feta cheese
⅓ cup chopped Italian parsley
¼ cup chopped fresh dill
sea salt
freshly ground black pepper
Greek yogurt, to serve

WILD GREENS IN AYVALIK

Even though I spend several months in Turkey, somehow I only manage to get to the coast once. An oversight really, as the country is bordered by no less than four seas — the Black, the Aegean, the Mediterranean and the Marmara. The coastal foray I do manage is to the pretty fishing village of Ayvalik on the northwest Aegean coast. For once I'm not solo, I've joined a tour. I hate group travel with a red-hot passion but since this is a Slow Food group from Istanbul, I figure the experience could be quite instructional.

The trip has been arranged so we can find out all about the wild greens harvest that happens here over the spring and summer months. All over the coast and in the hinterland, local women forage for a rich variety of plants that most of us would dismiss as weeds. There are dozens of types of edible wild greens here and people in these parts have long relied on them for a much-needed vitamin kick after a winter with little fresh produce. We stop for lunch at the home of one of the local olive oil producers and while we relax outside, we observe a local lady who is busy rummaging under some trees. Armed with just a small knife, she sweeps through the grass, regularly pausing to cut free some green plant and deposit it into a large bag. Within twenty minutes the bag is full of all manner of "weeds" — there are dozens of varieties. She tells us she cooks them all separately, boiling them for fifteen minutes or so, and then dresses them with yogurt or with garlic, lemon juice and olive oil to serve as a salad. They grow everywhere, she says, gesturing broadly around the area. I'm in awe of her abilities — everything growing underfoot looks unpromising to me.

Later, when we visit the Ayvalik market, the richness of this wild harvest falls into sharper focus. There are indeed dozens of types of these interesting greens for sale, piled high amid the more expected artichokes, leeks and carrots. There's wild fennel, wild mustard greens, mallow, samphire, wild chicory and nettles. There are wild radish greens, wild garlic, wild asparagus, various types of thistle, wild sorrel and dock. Some are used in salads while others, I'm told, are used for cooking in soups or incorporated into fillings for börek, omelettes or *bazlama*, a type of filled flat bread cooked on a griddle.

Wandering through these markets and sampling foods that I've never tasted before is simply one of my favorite things to do in the world. Even among complete strangers.

VEGETABLES AND SALADS 97

One of the most famous dishes in the extensive Turkish eggplant repertoire, the name of this dish literally means "the imam fainted." Supposedly he fainted on account of the expense of the ingredients (most likely the copious quantity of olive oil). This is great served as a meze.

IMAM BIYALDI

INGREDIENTS

2 lb 4 oz baby eggplants

1 cup extra virgin olive oil

3 large onions, thinly sliced

3 garlic cloves, chopped

1 lb 2 oz firm, ripe tomatoes

2 tablespoons chopped fresh dill,
    plus extra for serving

2 tablespoons chopped Italian parsley

sea salt

freshly ground black pepper

$\frac{1}{4}$ cup freshly squeezed lemon juice

$2\frac{1}{2}$ teaspoons sugar

METHOD

Using a vegetable peeler, peel strips from the eggplant at $\frac{3}{4}$-inch intervals to give a striped effect. Cut a very deep slit along the length of each eggplant, taking care not to cut all the way through and leaving both ends intact. Submerge the eggplants in a large bowl of salted water, using a plate to keep them submerged, and let stand for 20–30 minutes. Drain well and pat dry with paper towels.

Heat 2 tablespoons of the olive oil in a large saucepan over medium-low heat. Add the onion and garlic and cook for 7–8 minutes, or until softened. Remove from the heat and cool.

Cut a small cross in the base of each tomato and blanch them in a saucepan of boiling water for 1–2 minutes. Drain and plunge immediately into a bowl of cold water. Drain well, then peel and discard the skins and seeds, and finely chop the flesh. Combine with the onion mixture, dill and parsley in a bowl and season with salt and pepper.

Heat another 2 tablespoons of the oil in a large, deep frying pan over medium heat — the pan should be large enough to fit the eggplants in a single layer. Add the eggplants and cook for 7–8 minutes, turning often, until slightly softened. Remove the eggplants and cool.

Push the tomato and onion mixture into the slits in each eggplant so they are completely filled, then place the stuffed eggplant back into the frying pan. Scatter the remaining onion mixture over the top of the eggplants with the lemon juice, sugar and remaining oil. Add $\frac{1}{4}$ cup water to the pan and bring to a simmer over low heat. Cover the pan with a tight-fitting lid and cook for 60–70 minutes, or until the eggplants are tender. Remove from the heat and cool to room temperature. Scatter the extra dill and serve. **SERVES 6**

TOPIK

METHOD

Cook the chickpeas in boiling salted water for 45 minutes, or until tender. Drain well, reserving $\frac{1}{3}$ cup of the cooking liquid. When the chickpeas are cool, rub them vigorously in a clean dish towel to loosen the skins, removing as many as you can — this will improve the texture of the dish.

Combine the chickpeas, reserved cooking liquid and $\frac{1}{3}$ cup of the olive oil in a food processor and pulse until smooth, scraping the sides a few times — you may need to do this in batches. Press the potatoes through a potato ricer or mash well and add to the chickpea mixture, using the pulse button to process until just combined. Season with salt and pepper and set aside.

Heat the remaining oil in a saucepan over medium heat. Add the onion and garlic and cook for 6–7 minutes, or until softened. Add the raisins, pistachios, spices and tahini and cook for 2 minutes, stirring well, until fragrant. Remove from the heat and cool, then season with salt and pepper and stir in the parsley.

Lightly grease the base and side of a loaf pan with oil. Place half of the chickpea mixture into the pan, pressing to form an even layer, then add all of the onion mixture to create a second layer. Smooth the remaining chickpea mixture on top. Cover in plastic wrap and refrigerate for at least 3 hours or overnight. To serve, turn the topik out of the mould and cut into slices. **SERVES 6-8**

INGREDIENTS

$1\frac{1}{4}$ cups dried chickpeas,
    soaked overnight and drained

$\frac{1}{2}$ cup extra virgin olive oil,
    plus extra for greasing

12 oz all-purpose potatoes,
    peeled, halved and boiled

sea salt

freshly ground black pepper

2 onions, finely chopped

2 garlic cloves, crushed

$\frac{1}{3}$ cup raisins, chopped

$\frac{1}{3}$ cup shelled pistachios, chopped

$\frac{1}{2}$ teaspoon ground cinnamon

$\frac{1}{2}$ teaspoon ground allspice

2 tablespoons tahini

$2\frac{1}{2}$ tablespoons chopped Italian parsley

VINEGARED RAINBOW CHARD

METHOD

Cut the chard stems into $\frac{1}{2}$-inch-thick pieces. Tear the leaves into large pieces and set aside.

Heat the olive oil in a large saucepan over medium–low heat, add the chopped stems, garlic and cumin and cook for 5 minutes, or until softened. Increase the heat to medium-high, add the chard leaves and vinegar, cover the pan, and cook for 3–4 minutes, or until the leaves have wilted. Remove from the heat, strain off as much liquid as possible, set the vegetables aside and keep warm. Return the cooking juices to the pan and simmer for 4–5 minutes, or until the liquid has reduced. Place the chard in a bowl; season with salt and pepper. Serve warm or at room temperature with the reduced cooking liquid drizzled over the top. **SERVES 6-8**

INGREDIENTS

$3\frac{1}{4}$ lb rainbow chard, stalks
    trimmed, rinsed and dried

$\frac{1}{3}$ cup extra virgin olive oil

3 garlic cloves, thinly sliced

1 teaspoon cumin seeds

$\frac{1}{3}$ cup red wine vinegar

sea salt

freshly ground black pepper

YOGURT AND WALNUT-STUFFED EGGPLANT WITH TOMATO AND POMEGRANATE SAUCE

TOMATO AND POMEGRANATE SAUCE

$2\frac{1}{4}$ lb firm, ripe tomatoes

$\frac{1}{4}$ cup extra virgin olive oil

2 onions, finely chopped

3 garlic cloves, finely chopped

$1\frac{1}{2}$ tablespoons tomato paste

3 teaspoons superfine sugar

1 cinnamon stick

1 tablespoon pomegranate molasses
    (see note page 25)

sea salt

freshly ground black pepper

2 large eggplants

$1\frac{1}{2}$ tablespoons salt

olive oil, for cooking

$2\frac{2}{3}$ cups baby spinach leaves

7 oz goat's curd

1 cup Greek yogurt

1 garlic clove, finely chopped

$\frac{1}{3}$ cup walnut halves, finely chopped

$\frac{1}{2}$ bunch Italian parsley, finely chopped

TOMATO AND POMEGRANATE SAUCE

Cut a small cross in the base of each tomato and blanch them in a saucepan of boiling water for 1–2 minutes. Drain and plunge immediately into a bowl of cold water. Drain well, then peel and discard the skins and finely chop the flesh.

Heat the olive oil in a saucepan over medium heat. Add the onion and garlic and cook for 4–5 minutes, or until softened. Add the tomato paste and cook, stirring, for 1 minute, then add the tomato, sugar and cinnamon. Bring to a simmer, then reduce the heat to low and cook for about 30 minutes, or until the sauce has thickened. Remove from the heat and cool to room temperature. Remove the cinnamon stick and stir in the pomegranate molasses; season with salt and pepper. Set aside until ready to serve.

Cut the eggplants lengthwise into $\frac{5}{8}$-inch-thick slices. Place the slices in layers in a large colander, sprinkling each layer lightly with salt. Stand over a sink for 30 minutes, then rinse well and pat dry with paper towels. Heat a grill or griddle pan to medium. Brush the eggplant slices liberally with olive oil, then cook, in batches, for 2–3 minutes on each side, or until charred and golden. Remove the cooked eggplant to a large plate and cool to room temperature.

Meanwhile, place the spinach leaves in a saucepan, cover with a tight-fitting lid and cook over medium-high heat for 2–3 minutes, or until just wilted. Transfer to a colander and cool to room temperature. Using your hands, press firmly on the spinach to remove as much excess liquid as possible. Finely chop the spinach and place in a bowl with the goat's curd, yogurt, garlic, walnuts and parsley, stirring well to combine; season with salt and pepper.

Working with one eggplant slice at a time, place on a clean work surface with the short side facing you. Place a heaped tablespoon of the filling mixture in a thick line along one edge, then roll lengthwise to form a neat roll. Repeat with the remaining eggplant slices and filling.

Place the rolls on a serving platter and spoon the cooled sauce over the top. Serve immediately. (The rolls can be made in advance, covered with plastic wrap and refrigerated for up to 6 hours and then sauced just before serving. Sauce can be made up to 2 days in advance; keep in an airtight container in the refrigerator and bring to room temperature before serving.) **SERVES 6**

LENTIL, MINT AND FETA SALAD WITH POMEGRANATE DRESSING

POMEGRANATE DRESSING

Dry-fry the cumin seeds in a heavy-based frying pan over low heat, shaking the pan for 2 minutes, or until fragrant. Use a mortar and pestle to coarsely grind the cumin seeds, then combine in a bowl with the garlic, pomegranate molasses, sugar and chili flakes, whisking well to combine. Whisking constantly, add the olive oil in a slow, steady stream, then whisk in the lemon juice. Season with salt and pepper and set aside.

Put the lentils in a saucepan and add enough cold water to just cover. Bring to a boil, then reduce the heat to low, partially cover the pan, and cook the lentils for 25–30 minutes, or until just tender — take care not to overcook the lentils or they will be mushy. Drain well and cool to room temperature.

Meanwhile, heat a griddle pan to medium. Cut the onions in half lengthwise then cut each half into $\frac{1}{4}$-inch-thick wedges. Gently combine the onion with the oil, tossing well to coat. Cook the onions, in batches, for 3–4 minutes on each side, or until tender and lightly charred. Remove from the heat and cool.

Combine the cooled lentils, onion, walnuts, olives, parsley and mint in a large bowl and add the spinach leaves; season with salt and pepper. Toss gently to combine. Divide among serving bowls, top with the feta and drizzle the dressing over the top just before serving. **SERVES 4–6**

POMEGRANATE DRESSING

1 teaspoon cumin seeds
2 garlic cloves, very finely chopped
1 tablespoon pomegranate molasses
    (see note page 25)
$\frac{1}{2}$ teaspoon superfine sugar
1 large pinch dried chili flakes
$\frac{1}{2}$ cup extra virgin olive oil
2 teaspoons freshly squeezed lemon juice
sea salt
freshly ground black pepper

$1\frac{3}{4}$ cups brown or green lentils
2 red onions, peeled with root ends left intact
$2\frac{1}{2}$ tablespoons olive oil
$\frac{1}{2}$ cup walnut halves, coarsely chopped
$\frac{1}{2}$ cup pitted green olives, rinsed
1 handful Italian parsley, leaves chopped
    (optional)
1 cup mint leaves
$2\frac{1}{4}$ cups baby spinach leaves
7 oz feta cheese

This is a typical example of a Turkish vegetable dish, which uses a copious quantity of olive oil to intensify the divine flavors of the main vegetable components and fresh herbs. It is best served at room temperature.

ARTICHOKES, CELERIAC AND CARROTS IN OLIVE OIL

METHOD

Strip the tough outer leaves from the artichokes, then using a sharp knife, cut off the top of each artichoke, right down to the top of the heart. Carefully trim back the outer layers of each artichoke to expose the heart. Using a teaspoon, scrape out the hairy choke. Place the prepared artichokes into a bowl of acidulated water (see note).

Bring a saucepan of salted water to a boil. Add 2 tablespoons of the lemon juice and the flour, stirring well, then add the artichoke and onions, reserving the acidulated water in the bowl. Cover the pan and simmer for 5 minutes, then drain well.

Peel the celeriac and cut into $\frac{3}{4}$-inch pieces, placing them into the reserved acidulated water.

Place all the vegetables in a large saucepan. Add the stock, olive oil, sugar, thyme, bay leaf and $\frac{1}{4}$ cup of the lemon juice. Place a piece of parchment paper over the vegetables, then cover the pan with a lid. Bring to a simmer and cook over low heat for 30 minutes, or until the vegetables are very tender. Cool to room temperature in the liquid.

Transfer to a serving dish, season with salt and pepper, and a little extra lemon juice, if needed. **SERVES 6**

Note: Acidulated water is made by squeezing the juice of 1 lemon into a large bowl of water. It is used to help prevent certain fruits and vegetables from turning brown before cooking.

INGREDIENTS

8 globe artichokes, stems trimmed to
   $1\frac{1}{4}$ inches from base of artichoke
$\frac{1}{2}$ cup freshly squeezed lemon juice
3 teaspoons all-purpose flour
8 pickling onions, peeled, leaving root end
   intact, then halved
$1\frac{1}{2}$ lb celeriac
1 lb baby carrots, trimmed
   and halved lengthwise
$1\frac{1}{3}$ cups chicken stock
1 cup extra virgin olive oil
$2\frac{1}{2}$ teaspoons superfine sugar
3 thyme sprigs
1 fresh bay leaf
sea salt
freshly ground black pepper

TURLUTURLU

INGREDIENTS

$3/4$ cup dried chickpeas, soaked
    overnight and drained

1 large eggplant, trimmed and cut
    into $1\frac{1}{2}$-inch pieces

sea salt

$\frac{1}{2}$ cup extra virgin olive oil

3 garlic cloves, chopped

2 teaspoons ground coriander

2 teaspoons ground cumin

1 teaspoon dried chili flakes, or to taste

1 tablespoon sugar

2 red onions, cut into $1\frac{1}{4}$-inch pieces

14 oz all-purpose potatoes, cut into
    $1\frac{1}{4}$-inch pieces

1 large red bell pepper, seeded,
    ribs removed and cut into $1\frac{1}{2}$-inch pieces

1 lb 7 oz winter squash, peeled,
    seeded and cut into $1\frac{1}{4}$-inch pieces

3 zucchini, trimmed, halved
    lengthwise and cut into $1\frac{1}{2}$-inch pieces

2 cups tomato passata (puréed tomatoes)

1 cup cilantro leaves, chopped

METHOD

Cook the chickpeas in boiling salted water for 45 minutes, or until tender. Drain well.

Put the eggplant in a colander, sprinkling lightly with salt, and set aside for 30 minutes to drain. Rinse well, then pat dry on paper towels.

Preheat the oven to 350°F. Combine the olive oil, garlic, coriander, cumin, chili flakes and sugar in a large bowl and whisk well to combine. Add the eggplant, onion, potato and bell pepper to the bowl and toss to coat. Divide the mixture between two baking dishes, spreading evenly over the base and drizzling over any oil left in the bowl. Cook for 35 minutes, then add the squash and zucchini and cook for another 25 minutes, or until the vegetables are very tender and some are starting to char slightly. Scatter over the chickpeas, pour over the tomato passata and continue cooking for 5–10 minutes, or until heated through. Scatter with the cilantro and serve hot, warm or at room temperature. **SERVES 6**

TAKING TEA ON CUNDA ISLAND

I'm in Ayvalik, a seaside town on the Aegean coast, when I decide to take a short break from the tour group I've been with for the past few days. I decide to spend the morning at the market in Ayvalik sampling cheese, then I'm going to steal away to Cunda Island for some afternoon respite.

Before I head out of town I learn that Ayvalik cheeses are legendarily good and one of our group, a high-profile chef with a restaurant in the posh Istanbul suburb of Nişantasi, stocks up for her menu. I love the *köy peynir*, a young cow's milk cheese with a delicate, slightly flowery taste. My favorite quickly becomes *Lor peynir*, somewhat similar to ricotta but (dare I say this?) even better. It is a highly perishable fresh cheese that doesn't transport well and as a result is hard to find outside the area. It's creamy and rich and unbelievably smooth. I eat it as a light finish to lunch, served simply with homemade cherry jam and pekmez.

It's a kind of dessert that keeps me perfectly satisfied as I make my way to the slim causeway that joins the mainland near Ayvalik to Cunda Island. This is an idyllic spot that I soon learn, in season, is heaving with visitors — its minuscule population of two thousand triples during summer. I spend a blissful afternoon alone on Cunda, meandering up its winding old backstreets, where women sit knitting on stoops and kids kick balls against the walls of quaint old pastel-hued homes. From the hill that looms over the town there are views across the sea to Ayvalik and beyond. The waterfront promenade, packed with eateries, looks like the perfect spot for downing a raki or three and dining on seafood meze.

It's late in the afternoon and I venture into the Taş Kahve, a thoughtfully restored, 150-year-old tea house. The spacious interior features a high ceiling and lovely colored glass windows. This is a male domain where tea drinking, card playing and newspaper reading are the activities of choice. I love the way no one particularly cares if I'm here, so I can sip my tea in peace and people-watch. In my coat pocket I happily find a couple of cookies I'd forgotten were there — special mastic-flavored ones from a famous bakery in Ayvalik, made using olive oil and encrusted with sesame seeds. They're a regional specialty and are not too sweet; the perfect foil for the sugary tea. For a nanosecond I forget I'm expected back for dinner with the tour group. Right now I'm having a "Turkey moment": taking tea in some atmospheric old pile and eating something I've never seen before, even if it is something as simple as a cookie.

VEGETABLES AND SALADS 111

WHITE BEAN SALAD WITH TAHINI DRESSING AND GRILLED SHRIMP

INGREDIENTS

2 cups dried white beans,
    soaked overnight and drained

DRESSING

2 garlic cloves, crushed

¼ cup tahini

¼ cup freshly squeezed lemon juice

finely grated zest of 1 lemon

½ cup extra virgin olive oil

sea salt

freshly ground black pepper

1 large pinch dried chili flakes, or to
    taste (optional)

1 small red onion, very finely sliced

½ cup pitted green olives

1 cup Italian parsley leaves

2 tomatoes, cut into thin wedges

4 hard-boiled eggs, peeled and cut
    into quarters

36 raw shrimp, peeled
    and deveined, tails left intact

olive oil, for cooking

METHOD

Soak twelve wooden skewers in water for 30 minutes.

Put the beans in a saucepan and add just enough water to cover. Bring to a simmer and cook over medium-low heat for 50–60 minutes, or until very tender. Drain well and cool to room temperature.

DRESSING

Combine the garlic, tahini, lemon juice and lemon zest in a bowl. Whisking constantly, slowly add the olive oil in a thin stream, then stir in ¼ cup warm water until the dressing is a thick, creamy consistency. Season with salt, pepper and the chili flakes, then cover with plastic wrap and set aside.

Heat a grill or griddle pan to medium. Combine the beans and the dressing in a large bowl and toss well to coat. Add the onion, olives, parsley, tomato and egg and toss very gently to just combine.

Thread the shrimp onto skewers and brush all over with olive oil. Season well, then grill for about 4 minutes, turning once, until just cooked through. Divide the salad and shrimp skewers among serving plates and serve immediately. **SERVES 6**

VEGETABLES WITH BARLEY AND SPICED YOGURT

SPICED YOGURT

Heat the olive oil in a small saucepan over medium-low heat. Add the cumin, paprika and chili flakes and cook, stirring constantly, for 1–2 minutes, or until fragrant. Remove from the heat, transfer to a small bowl and cool to room temperature. Stir in the yogurt, pepper and salt. Cover with plastic wrap and refrigerate until needed.

Cook the barley in a saucepan of simmering water for 30 minutes, or until tender. Drain well and cool to room temperature.

Meanwhile, heat the oil in a large saucepan over medium-low heat. Add the onion, garlic and cinnamon and cook, for 4–5 minutes, or until softened. Add the carrot and celery and cook for 6–7 minutes, stirring regularly, until the vegetables have started to soften. Add the pepper paste and cook, stirring for 1 minute, then add the stock and bring to a simmer. Cover the pan and cook over medium-low heat for 10 minutes, or until the vegetables are very soft. Remove the cinnamon stick and discard.

Add the spinach, arugula, parsley and barley to the pan, stirring well to combine, then cover and cook for 3–4 minutes more, or until the greens have wilted. Remove from the heat and cool to room temperature. Season with salt and pepper. Transfer to a large serving dish and serve the barley and vegetables with the spiced yogurt. **SERVES 6**

SPICED YOGURT

$1\frac{1}{2}$ tablespoons extra virgin olive oil

2 teaspoons cumin seeds

2 teaspoons sweet paprika

$\frac{1}{2}$ teaspoon dried chili flakes, or to taste

2 cups sheep's milk yogurt

$\frac{1}{2}$ teaspoon freshly ground black pepper

1 teaspoon sea salt, or to taste

1 cup pearl barley

$\frac{1}{4}$ cup extra virgin olive oil

1 onion, finely chopped

2 garlic cloves, finely chopped

1 cinnamon stick

2 carrots, finely sliced

2 celery sticks, finely chopped

1 tablespoon Turkish pepper paste
    (see note page 13)

1 cup chicken stock

1 bunch spinach, stems trimmed, leaves
    rinsed, dried and coarsely chopped

1 bunch arugula, leaves rinsed,
    dried and coarsely chopped

1 cup Italian parsley leaves, chopped

sea salt

freshly ground black pepper

TOMATO, POMEGRANATE AND MINT SALAD WITH SAFFRON LABNEH

INGREDIENTS

1 pinch saffron threads

2 cups Greek yogurt

$2\frac{1}{4}$ lb mixed tomatoes

$2\frac{1}{2}$ teaspoons sugar

sea salt

freshly ground black pepper

1 pomegranate, seeds removed

$\frac{1}{4}$ cup mint leaves

2 tablespoons freshly squeezed lemon juice

$\frac{1}{4}$ cup extra virgin olive oil

METHOD

Stir the saffron into the yogurt, then spoon this mixture into a cheesecloth-lined sieve placed over a bowl. Place the yogurt in the refrigerator overnight to drain and thicken.

Cut the tomatoes into a variety of shapes — the larger ones into rounds, any egg tomatoes into wedges and the cherry and grape tomatoes into quarters. Arrange half of the tomatoes on a large platter, scatter with half of the sugar, season with salt and pepper, then scatter with half of the pomegranate seeds and mint leaves. On a second platter, repeat with the remaining tomatoes, sugar, pomegranate and mint. Drizzle the lemon juice and olive oil over both platters. Serve the salad with the yogurt mixture on the side. **SERVES 6**

GREEN TOMATO PICKLE

INGREDIENTS

2 cups white wine vinegar

2 garlic cloves, bruised

1 cinnamon stick

2 fresh bay leaves

2 teaspoons whole allspice berries

$\frac{1}{4}$ cup superfine sugar

$1\frac{1}{2}$ tablespoons sea salt

$1\frac{3}{4}$ lb green tomatoes, cut into
   $\frac{1}{2}$-inch wedges

METHOD

Combine the vinegar, garlic, cinnamon, bay leaves, allspice, sugar and salt in a saucepan with 1 cup water. Bring to a simmer, stirring regularly, until the sugar and salt have dissolved. Place all the tomato wedges in a 6-cup-capacity sterilized airtight jar and pour the mixture over the top to submerge the tomatoes — they should be just covered. Cool to room temperature, then seal the jar. Refrigerate for about 8 weeks before using. Green tomato pickle can be stored for 2–3 months in the refrigerator once opened. **MAKES 6 CUPS**

STUFFED EGGPLANT PICKLE

INGREDIENTS

$2\frac{1}{2}$ lb baby eggplants

6 garlic cloves, bruised

1 bunch fresh dill

2 teaspoons whole coriander seeds, crushed

$2\frac{1}{2}$ cups red wine vinegar

$\frac{1}{4}$ cup sugar

2 tablespoons sea salt

METHOD

Bring a saucepan of water to a simmer, add the eggplants and cook over medium-low heat for 6 minutes, or until softened. Drain well and set aside. Once cool, use a sharp knife to cut the eggplants lengthwise, leaving the stem end intact.

Combine the garlic, dill and coriander seeds in a bowl, then press into the cuts in each eggplant. Place the stuffed eggplants in a 6-cup-capacity sterilized airtight jar.

Mix together the vinegar, sugar and salt. Pour the vinegar mixture over the eggplants in the jar, seal, and set aside at room temperature for at least 3 weeks before using. Stuffed eggplant pickle can be stored for up to 3 months in the refrigerator once opened. **MAKES 6 CUPS**

BEET PICKLES IN CHERRY VINEGAR

METHOD

Cook the whole beet in boiling water for 30 minutes, or until tender. Drain well and cool slightly. When cool enough to handle, remove the beet skins and cut into halves. Place in a 5-cup-capacity sterilized airtight jar.

Combine the cinnamon, cloves, garlic, vinegar, sugar and salt in a saucepan with $1\frac{1}{2}$ cups water and bring to a simmer. Reduce the heat to low and cook for 6 minutes, stirring regularly. Pour the hot liquid over the beetroot in the jar and seal once cool. Keep in a cool dark place or in the refrigerator for at least 2 weeks before using. Beetroot pickles in cherry vinegar can be stored for 2–3 months in the refrigerator once opened. **MAKES 6 CUPS**

INGREDIENTS

$3\frac{1}{4}$ lb baby beets, trimmed and rinsed

2 cinnamon sticks, broken

2 teaspoons whole cloves

6 garlic cloves, bruised

2 cups cherry vinegar

$\frac{2}{3}$ cup superfine sugar

2 tablespoons sea salt

LEMON CARROT PICKLE

METHOD

Cook the carrots and lemon peel in a saucepan of salted boiling water for 2 minutes, then drain well. Place the carrot and lemon peel into a 5-cup-capacity sterilized airtight jar with the thyme.

Meanwhile combine the garlic, coriander seeds, lemon juice, vinegar, honey and $1\frac{1}{2}$ cups water in a saucepan and bring to a boil. Simmer over low heat for 3–4 minutes, then pour over the carrots in the jar and seal once cool. Stand in a cool dark place or in the refrigerator for at least 1 week before using. Lemon carrot pickle can be stored for 2–3 months in the refrigerator once opened. **MAKES 6 CUPS**

INGREDIENTS

$2\frac{1}{4}$ lb baby carrots, trimmed, peeled and halved lengthwise

2 lemons, peel removed in $\frac{1}{2}$-inch-wide strips, white pith removed

6 thyme sprigs

4 garlic cloves, bruised

$1\frac{1}{2}$ teaspoons coriander seeds

$\frac{3}{4}$ cup freshly squeezed lemon juice

$\frac{3}{4}$ cup white vinegar

$\frac{1}{3}$ cup honey

RICE AND BULGUR

Turkish rice is a variety called baldo and much of it is grown in north central Anatolia in and around Tosya. Grains are fat, somewhat like Italian arborio, and are used in various types of dolma (stuffed dishes) and in pilafs. Turkish cooks pride themselves on their ability to cook rice well — the grains should still be somewhat firm and separate, never sticky or clumped together. It is this pride in cooking simple things very, very well that exemplifies the spirit of the Turkish kitchen. Likewise, bulgur has had an important place on the table in Turkey since ancient times and is also fashioned into pilafs and salads.

PERDE PILAV

DOUGH

Sift the flour and salt into a bowl. In a separate bowl, combine the egg, yogurt, milk and olive oil and whisk until well combined. Add to the flour and stir to form a coarse dough. Turn the dough out onto a lightly floured surface and knead for 5 minutes, or until smooth, adding a little extra flour if the dough is too sticky. Roll the dough into a ball and place in a lightly oiled bowl, turning to coat. Cover with plastic wrap and set aside for 1 hour.

Meanwhile, coarsely chop one of the onions and place in a large saucepan with the chicken, carrot, celery and bay leaf. Add enough water to just cover the chicken, then cover the pan with a lid and slowly bring to a simmer over medium-low heat. Reduce the heat to very low and cook the chicken for 45 minutes, or until tender. Remove the chicken from the pan, then strain and reserve 3 cups of the stock, discarding the solids. Remove the meat from the chicken, discarding the skin and bones. Finely shred the meat using your hands and set aside.

Melt the butter in a large saucepan over medium heat. Chop the remaining onion and add to the pan with the chopped almonds and pine nuts and cook for 7–8 minutes, or until the onion has softened and the nuts are light golden. Add the rice, currants and allspice and cook, stirring, for 2–3 minutes, or until the rice is well coated and the mixture is fragrant. Add the reserved stock, bring to a simmer, then cover with a tight-fitting lid and cook over low heat for about 10–12 minutes, or until almost all the liquid has been absorbed — the rice will not be quite cooked through. Remove from the heat, stir in the dill and chicken, and season with salt and pepper. Set aside to cool.

Preheat the oven to 350°F and grease six $1\frac{3}{4}$-cup-capacity pie pans or oven-proof dishes. Place 3 of the extra whole almonds in the base of each. Divide the pastry into 6 even-sized pieces and roll out on a lightly floured surface to make circles big enough to line the pans, about $\frac{1}{2}$ inch thick. Use the pastry to line the pans, allowing any excess to overhang the edges — you will need to be careful not to tear the pastry as it is delicate. Spoon the rice mixture into the pans and fold over the excess pastry to cover the rice, pinching to seal. Bake in the oven for 50 minutes, or until the pastry is deep golden. Remove from the oven and cool in the pans for 5 minutes, then turn out and serve immediately with a green salad passed separately. **SERVES 6**

DOUGH

2 cups all-purpose flour

1 teaspoon sea salt

1 egg, lightly beaten

$\frac{1}{2}$ cup Greek yogurt

$\frac{1}{3}$ cup whole milk

$\frac{1}{4}$ cup olive oil

2 onions

$2\frac{3}{4}$ lb whole free-range chicken

1 carrot, chopped

1 celery stick, chopped

1 bay leaf

3 tablespoons butter, plus extra for greasing

$\frac{3}{4}$ cup blanched almonds, chopped, plus 18 whole almonds

$\frac{1}{3}$ cup pine nuts

2 cups long-grain white rice, rinsed and drained

$\frac{2}{3}$ cup currants, soaked in hot water for 30 minutes and drained

2 teaspoons ground allspice

1 bunch fresh dill, chopped

sea salt

freshly ground black pepper

BULGUR KÖFTE WITH TOMATO AND MINT SAUCE AND GARLIC YOGURT

GARLIC YOGURT

$1\frac{1}{2}$ cups Greek yogurt

2–3 garlic cloves, crushed

sea salt

freshly ground black pepper

TOMATO AND MINT SAUCE

$\frac{1}{4}$ cup extra virgin olive oil

1 large onion, finely chopped

3 garlic cloves, crushed

$1\frac{1}{2}$ teaspoons sweet paprika

$1\frac{1}{2}$ teaspoons dried mint

2 tablespoons tomato paste

$1\frac{1}{2}$ tablespoons Turkish pepper paste
   (see note page 13)

3 cups chicken or vegetable stock

$2\frac{1}{2}$ tablespoons freshly squeezed lemon
   juice, or to taste

sea salt

freshly ground black pepper

BULGUR KÖFTE

2 cups fine bulgur

$\frac{1}{4}$ cup fine semolina

$\frac{1}{3}$ cup all-purpose flour

$1\frac{1}{2}$ teaspoons ground cumin

$1\frac{1}{2}$ tablespoons Turkish pepper paste

$1\frac{1}{2}$ teaspoons sea salt

$1\frac{1}{2}$ teaspoons freshly ground black pepper

GARLIC YOGURT

Combine the yogurt and garlic in a bowl, season with salt and pepper and stir well to combine. Cover with plastic wrap and refrigerate until needed.

TOMATO AND MINT SAUCE

Heat the olive oil in a saucepan over medium-low heat. Add the onion and garlic and cook for 5–6 minutes, or until softened. Add the paprika, mint, tomato paste and pepper paste and cook for 2–3 minutes, stirring until fragrant. Add the stock and bring to a simmer, then reduce the heat to low, cover and cook for 5–6 minutes, stirring occasionally until smooth and thickened slightly. Stir in the lemon juice and season with salt and pepper.

BULGUR KÖFTE

Put the bulgur in the bowl of an electric mixer fitted with a beater attachment. Add 1 cup lukewarm water. Leave to soak for 5–6 minutes, or until all of the water has been absorbed. Add the semolina, flour, cumin, pepper paste, salt and pepper. Beat the mixture slowly, while gradually adding another 1 cup water. Continue to beat slowly until soft and well combined. (Alternatively, you can mix the köfte in a large bowl and knead using your hands for 10–12 minutes until elastic.) Taking a heaped 1 teaspoon of the mixture at a time, form into small balls, then use the tip of your little finger to make a small indentation in each ball.

Cook the köfte in a large saucepan of salted boiling water for 3–4 minutes, or until cooked through, then remove with a slotted spoon and keep warm while cooking the remaining köfte. Divide between serving dishes, spoon over the tomato and mint sauce and serve immediately with the garlic yogurt passed separately. **SERVES 4–6**

ICLI KÖFTE

FILLING

Heat the olive oil in a frying pan over medium heat. Add the onion, lamb, garlic and walnuts and cook for about 15 minutes, breaking up the meat, until the liquid has evaporated and the meat is browned. Stir in the raisins and allspice, and cook for 1 minute, then remove to a bowl and cool. Season with salt and pepper, then set aside.

Preheat the oven to 400°F. Place the bulgur in a bowl and add just enough cold water to cover, then set aside for 10 minutes. Drain well in a fine sieve, pressing down with your hands to remove as much liquid as possible.

Combine the bulgur, lamb and onion in a food processor and process until well combined. Season with salt and pepper, then continue to process until the mixture feels elastic. Place a bowl of cold water on the work surface to wet your hands — this will prevent the mixture sticking to your hands as you work. With damp hands, take a mounded 1 tablespoon of the mixture at a time and roll into a ball. Use your thumb to make an indentation deep into the ball, then use your hands to work the ball into a tall cup shape, making the sides as even and thin as you can without breaking them. Place 2 teaspoons of the filling mixture into the cavity of each, then close the bulgur mixture around the filling, forming a torpedo-shaped kibbeh. Repeat with the remaining bulgur mixture and filling — you should make about 20 in total.

Drizzle the oil over the base of a large baking dish, then arrange the kibbeh in a single layer in the base. Bake in the oven for 15 minutes, then turn the kibbeh over and bake for a further 10–15 minutes, or until golden and cooked through. Serve hot, warm or at room temperature with a green salad. **SERVES 6**

FILLING

$1\frac{1}{2}$ tablespoons olive oil

1 onion, finely chopped

9 oz ground lamb

2 garlic cloves, finely chopped

$\frac{1}{4}$ cup walnuts, chopped

$\frac{1}{4}$ cup raisins, chopped

$\frac{1}{2}$ teaspoon ground allspice

sea salt

freshly ground black pepper

$1\frac{1}{3}$ cups fine bulgur

14 oz ground lamb

2 tablespoons grated onion

sea salt

freshly ground black pepper

$\frac{1}{4}$ cup olive oil, for cooking

STREET LIFE IN DIYARBAKIR

I knew I'd love Diyarbakir even before I saw it for the first time. It's an ancient city with a five-thousand-year history of continuous habitation. It lies on the edge of the great, fertile Mesopotamian Plain to the country's southeast, right near the mighty Tigris River. Its historic old center is hemmed in by some six kilometers of brooding, basalt defensive walls.

The vernacular you hear on the streets of Diyarbakir is more likely to be Kurmanci than Turkish, and Kurdish cultural and intellectual activities are very much alive and kicking in the core of the city, which comprises a tight warren of ancient alleyways, complete with old mosques, churches and an energetic street life. There's some domestic tourism, but many Turks are anxious to avoid the place, as it was the scene of bloody tension between the outlawed PKK (Kurdistan Workers' Party) and the Turkish armed forces in the latter part of the 1990s — in fact, emergency rule was only lifted in the city in 2002. In the surrounding countryside, there's still a heavy army presence.

Compared to the slicker, more wealthy parts of Turkey, Diyarbakir still has a raw, in-your-face immediacy. Nowhere is this more profoundly expressed than in the food. Here, things aren't so sanitized. Yogurt is delivered to shops in big metal buckets, often left uncovered. Women congregate in narrow streets and roast whole eggplants over little wood fires that fill the neighborhood with smoke. From a wall-top vantage point, I can look over the city in the late summer and see big tubs of bell pepper purée evaporating slowly into a dense, rich paste in the blazing heat. The streets are a crush of humanity and the alleyways are the domain of children. Flat-roofed houses are festooned with strings of chilies and tomatoes drying in the sun to make ready for wintertime use. At the famed cheese market, big fat lengths of the local plaited cheese lie in briny baths, exposed to the ambient temperature.

On one corner a man stands all day, mixing tubs of ciğ köfte using his bare hands. Once cooked, he spreads the ground meat over squares of flat bread, scatters over some herbs and radishes and drenches it in pomegranate molasses, selling it, rolled neatly in yesterday's newspaper, for a few Turkish lira. Elsewhere, men fan kebab stands into life and young boys sell frothy copper cups of cold *ayran* to parched passers-by. Legions of men lounge in the afternoon sun drinking tea and smoking, while young simit sellers weave in and out, dispensing their wares to the hungry.

SQUASH TRAY KÖFTE

OREGANO-PAPRIKA ROASTED TOMATOES

Preheat the oven to 350°F. Put the tomatoes in a single layer in the base of a roasting dish and sprinkle with the sugar, spices and oregano leaves. Drizzle the olive oil and vinegar over the top, season with salt and pepper and cook for 1 hour, or until the tomatoes are soft and slightly charred around the edges.

FILLING

Heat the olive oil in a large frying pan over medium-high heat. Add the lamb, onion and garlic and cook for 7–8 minutes, stirring often to break up the meat. Add the tomato paste, allspice, cinnamon and chili flakes and cook, stirring, for another 2 minutes. Remove from the heat and stir in the chopped walnuts and parsley, then set aside to cool.

Place the bulgur in a bowl and add just enough cold water to cover, then leave to soak for 10 minutes. Drain well in a fine sieve, pressing with your hands to remove as much liquid as possible.

Heat 1 tablespoon of the olive oil in a small saucepan over medium heat. Add the squash, cover, and cook for 15 minutes, stirring occasionally until the squash is very tender. Remove from the heat, drain off any excess liquid and stir the squash well to form a coarse purée; cool to room temperature.

Put the lamb, onion, allspice and chili flakes in the bowl of an electric mixer fitted with a paddle attachment and mix on low speed for 5 minutes, or until a little sticky. Add the bulgur, puréed squash, salt and pepper, and mix for 5–6 minutes more, or until well combined and elastic. (Alternatively, you can mix the köfte in a large bowl and knead using your hands for 10–12 minutes until elastic.)

Pour half of the remaining olive oil into the base of an 8-cup-capacity baking dish, then use your hands to spread half of the bulgur mixture evenly over the base of the dish. Scatter with the filling. Take small handfuls of the remaining bulgur mixture at a time and flatten them, then arrange them alongside each other to create an even layer over the filling. Using a large sharp knife, cut a diamond pattern in the top of the köfte. Press a walnut half into each diamond, then brush the remaining olive oil over the top of the köfte. Bake in the oven for 40 minutes, or until light golden and cooked through. Remove from the oven and cool slightly before serving warm or at room temperature with the lemon wedges and the roasted tomatoes passed separately. **SERVES 8**

OREGANO-PAPRIKA ROASTED TOMATOES

12 small tomatoes, halved lengthwise
$1\frac{1}{2}$ teaspoons superfine sugar
$1\frac{1}{2}$ teaspoons sweet paprika
$\frac{1}{2}$ teaspoon dried chili flakes
1 tablespoon oregano leaves
$2\frac{1}{2}$ tablespoons olive oil
$2\frac{1}{2}$ tablespoons red wine vinegar
sea salt
freshly ground black pepper

FILLING

2 tablespoons extra virgin olive oil
10 oz ground lamb
1 onion, finely chopped
2 garlic cloves, crushed
1 tablespoon tomato paste
$\frac{1}{2}$ teaspoon ground allspice
$\frac{1}{2}$ teaspoon ground cinnamon
1 teaspoon dried chili flakes
$\frac{1}{2}$ cup walnuts, chopped
$\frac{1}{3}$ cup chopped Italian parsley

2 cups fine bulgur
$\frac{1}{2}$ cup extra virgin olive oil
$1\frac{1}{4}$ lb winter squash, peeled, seeded and chopped
$1\frac{1}{2}$ lb ground lamb
1 onion, finely chopped
$\frac{1}{2}$ teaspoon ground allspice
1 teaspoon dried chili flakes
1 teaspoon sea salt
1 teaspoon freshly ground black pepper
16 walnut halves
lemon wedges, to serve

TOMATO, RAISIN AND WHEAT PILAF

MINTED YOGURT

2 cups Greek yogurt

1 garlic clove, finely chopped (optional)

3 tablespoons chopped mint

sea salt

freshly ground black pepper

$1\frac{1}{2}$ cups coarse bulgur

$\frac{1}{3}$ cup olive oil

2 onions, finely chopped

2 garlic cloves, crushed

$1\frac{1}{2}$ tablespoons tomato paste

$2\frac{1}{2}$ teaspoons ground cumin

$\frac{1}{4}$ cup chopped sun-dried tomatoes

$\frac{1}{3}$ cup white raisins (see note)

$2\frac{1}{4}$ cups chicken stock

$2\frac{1}{4}$ lb lamb leg roasts, trimmed

sea salt

freshly ground black pepper

lemon wedges, to serve

baby spinach salad, to serve

MINTED YOGURT

Combine the yogurt, garlic and mint in a bowl and season with salt and black pepper. Stir well to combine, then cover and refrigerate until needed.

Rinse the bulgur under running water and drain well. Heat $2\frac{1}{2}$ tablespoons of the olive oil in a large saucepan over medium heat. Add the onion and garlic and cook for 5–6 minutes, or until softened. Add the tomato paste, cumin, sun-dried tomato and white raisins and cook, stirring often, for 3–4 minutes, then add the bulgur. Stir to combine, then add the stock and bring to a simmer. Cover, reduce the heat to very low and cook for 15–20 minutes, or until most of the liquid has been absorbed. Remove the pan from the heat and set aside, covered, for 15 minutes, or until the bulgur is very tender.

Meanwhile, heat the remaining oil in a heavy-based frying pan over medium heat. Season the lamb leg roasts with salt and pepper and place in the pan. Cover the pan with a lid and cook the roasts for 25 minutes, turning once, until cooked through but still a little pink in the middle. Remove from the heat and rest the meat for 10 minutes before slicing.

Divide the pilaf, lamb, minted yogurt and lemon wedges among shallow bowls or plates and serve immediately with a spinach salad passed separately. **SERVES 6**

Note: Unlike most raisins, which are sun-dried, white raisins, or muscats, are dried in the oven. They are less sweet than golden raisins. You can use regular raisins if white raisins are unavailable.

WILD GREENS, FREEKH AND SHRIMP WITH SPICY BELL PEPPER PURÉE

BELL PEPPER PURÉE

Place the bell peppers directly over a low flame and cook, turning often, for 10–15 minutes, or until the skin is blackened all over. (Alternatively, cook the peppers on a grill heated to high.) Transfer to a bowl, cover with a dish towel and stand until cool enough to handle. Using your hands, remove the blackened skins and seeds, using a little water to loosen if necessary — do not rinse them in water or you will lose flavor. Tear the pepper flesh into pieces and set aside.

Heat the olive oil in a saucepan over medium heat. Add the onion and garlic and cook for 6–7 minutes, or until softened. Add the pepper paste, paprika, chili flakes and cinnamon and cook, stirring, for 2 minutes. Remove from the heat and transfer to a food processor. Add the peppers and sugar and process to make a coarse purée. Season with salt and pepper and refrigerate until needed — bring it back to room temperature before serving.

Put the freekh and $1\frac{1}{2}$ cups water in a saucepan and bring to a simmer, cover and cook over low heat for 25–30 minutes, or until the water has been absorbed and the freekh is tender. Remove from the heat and set aside.

Remove any tough stems from the cabbage and spinach. Wash all of the greens and drain. Heat half of the olive oil in a very large saucepan, add the garlic and cinnamon stick and cook over medium heat for 2 minutes, or until fragrant. Add the cabbage and $\frac{1}{3}$ cup water, increase the heat to medium-high, cover and cook for 7–8 minutes, stirring occasionally until tender. Remove to a bowl.

Heat the remaining oil in the same pan and add the spinach, arugula, watercress, dandelion leaves (if using) and shrimp. Cook, stirring often, for 3–4 minutes, or until the greens have wilted and the shrimp are nearly cooked through. Return the cabbage to the pan with the freekh, stir well to combine, then cover and cook for 3 minutes, or until heated through. Season with salt and pepper and discard the cinnamon stick. Serve immediately with the pepper purée passed separately. **SERVES 6**

Note: Freekh is an Arabic food that's eaten in the south of Turkey, where there is a strong Middle Eastern influence. It is a form of wheat, picked while still green, that is then roasted and sun-dried to give it a fantastic smoky flavor.

SPICY BELL PEPPER PURÉE

3 large red bell peppers

$2\frac{1}{2}$ tablespoons olive oil

1 large onion, finely chopped

3 garlic cloves, chopped

$1\frac{1}{2}$ tablespoons Turkish pepper paste
 (see note page 13)

$1\frac{1}{2}$ teaspoons sweet paprika

$1\frac{1}{2}$ teaspoons dried chili flakes

$\frac{1}{2}$ teaspoon ground cinnamon

1 teaspoon sugar

sea salt

freshly ground black pepper

1 cup freekh (green wheat),
 rinsed well

1 head Tuscan cabbage

9 oz spinach

4 cups arugula

10 oz watercress

4 cups dandelion leaves (optional)

$\frac{1}{3}$ cup extra virgin olive oil

3 garlic cloves, crushed

1 cinnamon stick

$3\frac{1}{3}$ lb raw large shrimp,
 peeled and deveined

CHICKEN BILBER DOLMAS

CHICKEN FILLING

$\frac{1}{3}$ cup extra virgin olive oil

1 onion, finely chopped

1 garlic clove, finely chopped

2 tablespoons pine nuts

$1\frac{1}{2}$ cups long-grain white rice

2 boneless, skinless chicken thighs,
    trimmed and finely chopped

2 teaspoons Turkish pepper paste
    (see note page 13)

2 tablespoons currants

$1\frac{1}{2}$ teaspoons superfine sugar

$\frac{1}{4}$ teaspoon ground cinnamon

$\frac{1}{4}$ teaspoon ground allspice

$\frac{1}{2}$ teaspoon sea salt

$1\frac{1}{4}$ cups chicken stock

$1\frac{1}{2}$ tablespoons freshly squeezed
    lemon juice

freshly ground black pepper

6 green or red banana peppers or
    $5\frac{1}{2}$ oz small red bell peppers

CHICKEN FILLING

Heat half of the olive oil in a saucepan over medium heat. Add the onion, garlic and pine nuts and cook for 5–6 minutes, or until the onion has softened. Add the rice and cook, stirring, for 2 minutes, then add the chicken, pepper paste, currants, sugar, cinnamon, allspice, salt and half of the chicken stock. Bring to a simmer, cover with a tight-fitting lid and cook over low heat for 10 minutes, or until the liquid has been absorbed. Stir in the lemon juice and season with pepper. Remove from the heat and cool slightly.

Cut the tops off the peppers and reserve. Using a teaspoon, remove the seeds and ribs from the peppers and discard. Stuff the peppers with the chicken filling, taking care not to fill them to the top as the rice needs room to expand. Replace the tops of the peppers, then lay them in a deep frying pan so they fit snugly in a single layer. Pour the remaining stock and oil into the pan and cover with a sheet of parchment paper. Place a plate over the top to gently weigh them down and cover with a lid. Place over low heat and cook for 45–50 minutes, or until the peppers are tender and the filling is cooked. Serve warm or at room temperature with the cooking liquid spooned over the top.
MAKES 6

BULGUR PILAF

INGREDIENTS

2 cups coarse bulgur

$2\frac{1}{2}$ tablespoons olive oil

1 large onion, finely chopped

1 garlic clove, crushed

1 cinnamon stick

3 cups chicken stock

sea salt

freshly ground black pepper

METHOD

Wash the bulgur under cold running water until the water runs clear, then drain well and set aside.

Heat the olive oil in a large saucepan over medium heat. Add the onion and garlic and cook for 5–6 minutes, stirring often until softened. Add the cinnamon stick and stock, bring to a boil, then reduce the heat to low, cover, and cook for about 12–15 minutes, or until all of the liquid has been absorbed. Season with salt and pepper; fluff the grains with a fork. Serve warm or at room temperature. **SERVES 4–6**

RICE PILAF

INGREDIENTS

2 cups baldo or other
medium-grain white rice (see note)

3 tablespoons butter

1 large onion, finely chopped

1 garlic clove, crushed

1 fresh bay leaf

3 cups chicken stock

sea salt

freshly ground black pepper

METHOD

Wash the rice under cold running water until the water runs clear, then drain well and set aside.

Melt the butter in a large saucepan over medium heat. Add the onion and garlic and cook for 5–6 minutes, stirring often until softened. Add the drained rice and cook for 2–3 minutes, stirring to coat the rice and heat through. Add the bay leaf and stock, bring to a boil, then reduce the heat to low, cover, and cook for 12 minutes, or until all of the liquid has been absorbed. Remove from the heat and stand, covered, for 20 minutes more, or until the rice is tender. Season with salt and pepper; fluff the grains with a fork. Serve warm or at room temperature. **SERVES 4–6**

Note: Baldo rice is an Italian medium-grain rice. This rice variety is also grown in Turkey and is perfect for making pilafs and dolma fillings as it holds its shape well when cooked and is not sticky.

SWISS CHARD AND BULGUR PILAF WITH SPICED ONIONS

METHOD

Heat 2 tablespoons of the olive oil in a large, heavy-based frying pan over medium heat. Add the onion and cook for 15–18 minutes, or until deep golden. Add the allspice, paprika and chili flakes (if using), season with salt and pepper, and continue cooking for 1–2 minutes, or until fragrant. Remove from the heat and set aside until needed.

Remove the stems and any thick veins from the chard leaves, discarding any tough or damaged outer leaves. Trim $3/4$ inch from the ends of the stems, then finely chop the stems and veins. Rinse and dry the leaves, then finely chop them and set aside. Heat the remaining olive oil in a large saucepan over medium heat. Add the chopped chard stems to the pan, cover, and cook for 10 minutes, stirring often, until softened. Add the barberries, bulgur and stock to the pan, stirring well to combine, then bring the mixture to a simmer. Cover the pan and cook over low heat for about 15–20 minutes, or until the bulgur is almost tender. Remove from the heat and let stand for 5 minutes. Season with salt and pepper and fluff with a fork.

Meanwhile, fill a saucepan with about $1\frac{1}{4}$ inches water and bring to a boil. Add the reserved chard leaves, cover with a tight-fitting lid, and cook for 5 minutes, or until tender. Drain in a colander, cool, then use your hands to press down and extract as much liquid as possible. Combine in a bowl with the yogurt and garlic, season with salt and pepper, then cover with plastic wrap and refrigerate until needed.

Serve the pilaf warm or at room temperature with the spiced onions and yogurt mixture. **SERVES 6**

Note: Barberries are sour little fruits from a shrub, available from Middle Eastern grocery stores. They lend a pretty pink color and refreshingly tart kick to dishes such as this pilaf.

INGREDIENTS

$\frac{1}{3}$ cup extra virgin olive oil

3 large onions, thinly sliced

1 teaspoon ground allspice

1 teaspoon sweet paprika

1 teaspoon dried chili flakes (optional)

sea salt

freshly ground black pepper

$1\frac{3}{4}$ lb Swiss chard

$\frac{1}{3}$ cup dried barberries
    (see note)

$1\frac{1}{2}$ cups coarse bulgur

2 cups chicken stock

$1\frac{1}{2}$ cups Greek yogurt

2 garlic cloves, crushed

MAKING PEKMEZ AND PESTIL IN THE COUNTRYSIDE

Pekmez is a defining ingredient of Turkish cooking — it's the molasses-like syrup that results from the boiling down of fruit must. It's thick, gooey and dark and, as a precursor of sugar, is an ancient food. A variety of fruits are used for pekmez, such as pears, mulberries, plums, figs and even carob. But arguably the most common type is made from grapes. Pekmez is used to flavor fruit compotes and rustic desserts, such as flour halva, and is eaten, with tahini, for breakfast with bread. I learned it is also used medicinally, in much the same way balsamic vinegar is in Italy; a spoonful every morning is said to be good for whatever might ail you.

I'm in Diyarbakir in autumn when my friend Mehmet invites me to his parents' village about thirty kilometers away to see pekmez being made. We hop on a bus that will drop us nearby and end up walking the last few kilometers through the hot sun on dusty roads.

We soon forget how uncomfortable we are when we reach fields thick with wild thyme. Its sweet, piney fragrance is released with every footfall. We're quite elevated here and enjoy sweeping vistas of agricultural land. Our path turns through grape vines as we approach Mehmet's mom, dad, and various other relatives who are hard at work making pestil, a dried, leathery fruit paste. For this, grapes have been boiled down to a thick purée, strained and then spread thinly and evenly over sheets of cloth. These are left to dry in the sun until the fruit has a pliable, leathery texture. Then it is cut into manageable pieces and put aside for use as a sustaining snack for the year ahead. It takes five people to make it; one person holds each of the corners of the cloth while the fifth person spreads on the paste.

We then watch as the men take turns to stir the grape pulp that is slowly reducing down into pekmez. It cooks in an enormous cauldron set over a wood fire and while the process is simple, the work is hot, hard and goes on for hours. The family spends three days laboring here to get the pekmez and pestil made, using the same processes and equipment employed for centuries. It's a scene played out through much of rural Turkey year round and reminds me, along with other acts of preserving the harvest that I've seen (drying fruits and vegetables and making sun-dried pastes, for example), that in some parts of the country at least, there is still a reliance on what the seasons offer for food.

RICE AND BULGUR   143

Kisir is the tabouleh of Turkey, although it contains a good deal less parsley and has a lovely reddish hue from the vegetable paste, tomato and spices. To me it begs for the addition of rare-grilled tuna or salmon. In Turkey it is usually served as a meze or side dish with grilled lamb, beef or fish.

KISIR

INGREDIENTS

$1\frac{3}{4}$ lb tuna steaks

olive oil, for brushing

sea salt

freshly ground black pepper

2 cups fine bulgur

$\frac{1}{3}$ cup extra virgin olive oil,
   plus extra for cooking

1 onion, finely chopped

2 garlic cloves, crushed

1 tablespoon tomato paste

1 tablespoon Turkish pepper paste
   (see note page 13)

$1\frac{1}{2}$ teaspoons ground cumin

2 teaspoons dried chili flakes

3 firm, ripe tomatoes, finely chopped

2 small cucumbers, finely chopped

2 teaspoons dried mint

$1\frac{1}{2}$ tablespoons pomegranate molasses
   (see note page 25)

$2\frac{1}{2}$ tablespoons freshly squeezed lemon
   juice, or to taste

$\frac{1}{3}$ cup chopped Italian parsley

$\frac{1}{3}$ cup chopped mint leaves

lemon wedges, to serve

METHOD

Preheat a grill or griddle pan to medium-high. Brush the tuna steaks with the olive oil to coat and cook for about 2 minutes on each side, or until cooked through but still a little pink in the middle. Season with salt and pepper, then remove from the heat and allow to cool to room temperature. Break into large pieces and set aside.

Meanwhile, put the bulgur in a large bowl and pour over 2 cups boiling water. Cover and leave to soak for 10–15 minutes, or until the water has been absorbed.

Meanwhile, heat the extra virgin olive oil in a small frying pan over medium heat, add the onion and garlic and cook for 5–7 minutes, or until softened. Stir in the tomato paste and pepper paste, cumin and chili flakes, and cook for 2–3 minutes, or until fragrant. Remove from the heat, cool to room temperature, then stir the mixture into the bulgur. Add the tomato, cucumber, mint, pomegranate molasses and lemon juice, tossing to mix well. Add the tuna and toss gently to combine; season with salt and pepper, scatter with the parsley and mint leaves and serve immediately with lemon wedges on the side. **SERVES 6**

Mussels stuffed with rice are a popular street food in Istanbul. The flavors in this pilaf mirror those of the stuffed version, but the pilaf is much easier to make. You can eat this meal hot, but it actually tastes better at room temperature.

MUSSEL, DILL AND CURRANT PILAF

METHOD

Put the rice and salt in a bowl and pour over enough boiling water to cover. Set aside for 30 minutes to soak, then drain well.

Meanwhile, bring 2 cups water to a boil in a large saucepan. Add the mussels, cover, and cook for 2–3 minutes, shaking the pan occasionally, until the mussels have just opened; discard any that do not open after 5-6 minutes. Remove the mussels to a bowl, then strain and reserve the cooking liquid — add enough water to make 2 cups. When cool enough to handle, remove the mussel meat from the shells, cover and refrigerate until required.

Heat the oil in a large saucepan over medium heat. Add the onion and garlic and cook for 5–7 minutes, or until softened. Add the pine nuts, currants, allspice and rice and cook for 2–3 minutes, stirring well to combine, until the rice is heated through. Add the reserved mussel liquid and bring to a boil, stirring well. Reduce the heat to a simmer, cover, and cook for 15 minutes, or until the liquid has been absorbed. Remove from the heat and stand for 5 minutes. Add the mussels, stir well to combine, then cover and stand for another 5 minutes. Sprinkle with dill before serving. **SERVES 6**

INGREDIENTS

$1\frac{1}{2}$ cups baldo rice or other
    medium-grain white rice (see note
    page 140)

2 teaspoons sea salt

$3\frac{3}{4}$ lb black mussels, beards
    removed and shells scrubbed

$\frac{1}{4}$ cup extra virgin olive oil

1 large onion, finely chopped

2 garlic cloves, finely chopped

$\frac{1}{3}$ cup pine nuts, toasted

$\frac{1}{3}$ cup currants

$\frac{3}{4}$ teaspoon ground allspice

$\frac{1}{3}$ cup chopped fresh dill

FISH AND SEAFOOD

At many Turkish markets a dazzling array of fish, either bright-eyed and on ice, or still alive and thrashing in a tub of water, can be found. This bounty speaks of the miles of coastline strung around the Turkish borders where the Black, Marmara, Aegean and Mediterranean seas lap. Red mullet, trout, bonito, mackerel, sea bass, sea perch, tuna, swordfish and sardines are popular, as are squid and mussels. These are subject to the simplest of treatments — grilling or baking usually — and are served with unfussy accompaniments, leaving the fish tasting of the sea, river or stream from which it was plucked.

MACKEREL WITH ONIONS, APPLE CIDER VINEGAR, CUMIN AND CHICKPEAS

METHOD

Preheat the oven to 400°F. Cook the chickpeas in boiling salted water for 45 minutes, or until tender. Drain well.

Heat the olive oil in a large saucepan over medium heat. Add the onion, garlic and cumin seeds and cook for 6–7 minutes, or until softened. Add the stock, vinegar and chickpeas, then season with salt and pepper. Bring to a simmer, then reduce the heat to low and keep warm.

Arrange the mackerel in a single layer in a large baking dish and season with salt and pepper. Pour the hot chickpea mixture over, scatter with the chili flakes, then cover the dish tightly with foil. Bake in the oven for about 7–8 minutes, or until the fish is just cooked through. Serve with boiled potatoes and a green salad passed separately. **SERVES 6**

INGREDIENTS

1 cup dried chickpeas, soaked overnight and drained

$\frac{1}{4}$ cup extra virgin olive oil

3 large red onions, thinly sliced

2 garlic cloves, finely chopped

1 teaspoon cumin seeds, lightly crushed

2 cups fish or chicken stock

$\frac{1}{4}$ cup apple cider vinegar

sea salt

freshly ground black pepper

Six 6-oz mackerel fillets

1 teaspoon dried chili flakes, or to taste

SEMOLINA-CRUSTED WHITING WITH TOMATO, POMEGRANATE AND SUMAC RELISH

TOMATO, POMEGRANATE AND SUMAC RELISH

5 plum tomatoes, seeded and finely chopped

1 small red onion, finely chopped

$2\frac{1}{2}$ teaspoons superfine sugar

1 tablespoon pomegranate molasses (see note page 25)

1 tablespoon freshly squeezed lemon juice

1 teaspoon dried chili flakes

$1\frac{1}{2}$ teaspoons sumac

$\frac{1}{4}$ cup extra virgin olive oil

1 cup Italian parsley leaves, chopped

1 cup cilantro leaves, chopped

sea salt

freshly ground black pepper

$\frac{1}{2}$ cup polenta

12 whole whiting or other small firm white fish, cleaned

$\frac{1}{3}$ cup olive oil

lemon wedges, to serve

TOMATO, POMEGRANATE AND SUMAC RELISH

Combine all of the ingredients in a bowl, season with salt and pepper, then cover and stand at room temperature for 1 hour for the flavors to develop.

Put the polenta on a large flat plate and press the fish into the polenta, turning to coat evenly on both sides.

Heat the oil in a large nonstick frying pan over medium-low heat. Add the fish to the pan, laying them in a single layer and alternating heads to tails so they fit snugly. Cook for 6 minutes. Remove from the heat and place a flat tray over the top of the pan. Invert the pan carefully, so that the fish land on the tray, then carefully slide the fish back into the frying pan, taking care not to break the polenta coating. Cook for another 3–4 minutes, or until cooked through. Slide the fish onto serving plates and serve immediately with lemon wedges and the relish on the side. **SERVES 4**

Where would Turkey be without raki? This non-sweet, anise-flavored rocket fuel is the social lubricant of choice and is most enjoyed as an accompaniment to meze. It's unlikely that many Turks would cook with it, although it works extremely well here splashed over baked fish.

BAKED FISH WITH DILL BUTTER AND RAKI, ROASTED TOMATOES AND PINE NUTS

METHOD

Preheat the oven to 400°F. Combine the butter, dill, garlic, lemon zest and pepper in a bowl, and stir well to combine.

Using a large, sharp knife, cut four diagonal slits into the flesh of the fish on both sides. Place the butter mixture inside the slits. Place the fish side by side in a large roasting pan and season with salt. Scatter with the tomatoes and pine nuts (if using), then drizzle the raki over the fish. Bake in the oven for 20–25 minutes, or until the fish is just cooked through in the middle. Serve immediately with a green salad and flat bread passed separately. **SERVES 4**

INGREDIENTS

5 tablespoons butter, softened

$\frac{1}{2}$ cup chopped fresh dill

2 garlic cloves, crushed

$1\frac{1}{2}$ teaspoons finely grated lemon zest

1 teaspoon freshly ground black pepper

$\frac{3}{4}$ lb whole bream, snapper, barramundi or other firm white fish, cleaned

sea salt

$\frac{3}{4}$ lb small yellow tomatoes

$2\frac{1}{2}$ tablespoons pine nuts, lightly toasted (optional)

$\frac{1}{2}$ cup raki or ouzo

green salad, to serve

flat bread (page 63), to serve

A FERRY RIDE TO CIYA

I can't remember how I first discovered Ciya, the now famous restaurant in Kadikoy, on the Asian side of Istanbul. Its existence is hardly a secret — Chef Musa Dagdeverin is something of a culinary legend, not only in Turkey but overseas as well. All I know is, Ciya is my refueling stop of choice in Istanbul. Partly this is to do with the ferry trip required to get there. Taking a commuter ferry is one of the defining experiences of a trip to Istanbul. Complete with precarious gangplanks, wooden seats and decking, and roving hawkers dispensing glasses of hot tea, ferries are a constant presence on the Bosporus. They crisscross the water between some twenty-seven stops, ducking between fishing boats and oil tankers with a token entourage of gliding gulls constantly in tow. From a ferry deck the vistas of the city are spectacular.

While it is not a pretty place, Kadikoy bristles with energy and for a slice of "everyday" Istanbul it can't be topped. There are wide, busy streets flanked by banks and dull chain stores masking scruffy back lanes full of secondhand bookshops and antique stores. There are old mosques, a sprinkling of historic churches and even one of Istanbul's oldest synagogues, the Hemdat Israel. Kadikoy has a fabulous food market, too, strung out along Bahariye Caddesi. It's a lively place to wander around and try something new, such as the so-called mad honey from the Black Sea, olives from Bodrum, or new-season hazelnuts from Giresun.

Ciya is not one, but several neighboring restaurants. My favorite of these is Ciya Sofrasi, where the menu, which changes daily, is served in the casual style of a lokanta. A lokanta is a genre of restaurant common throughout Turkey where simple food is served from hot-water baths, ready to go. For some twenty-five years, Dagdeverin has been researching and documenting traditional dishes, including many in danger of dying out completely. Thus a meal at Ciya is something of an exercise in food anthropology — you dine here on fare you'd be hard pressed to find anywhere else. Over a thousand dishes are rotated through the kitchen each year so depending on the season there might be a chestnut, lamb, apple, onion and chickpea soup, lamb chops with quinces, loquats baked with lamb, stuffed spleen, or milk thistle braised with lamb and lemon. The sweet candied fruits and vegetables are legendary and the secret to their jewel-like transparency is a thorough soaking in limewater before cooking. I leave, as I always do, with a feeling of deep contentment and the promise to return.

FISH AND SEAFOOD 161

SALT-BAKED FISH WITH BEET SALAD AND PISTACHIO AND TAHINI SAUCE

BEET SALAD

$2\frac{1}{4}$ lb beets, trimmed and scrubbed clean

$1\frac{1}{4}$ cups olive oil

$\frac{1}{3}$ cup currants

2 garlic cloves, crushed

1 egg yolk

1 tablespoon dijon mustard

$\frac{1}{4}$ cup red wine vinegar

sea salt

freshly ground black pepper

$\frac{1}{2}$ cup semi-dried black olives

1 head radicchio, trimmed, tough outer
    leaves discarded, leaves torn

3 tablespoons cilantro, leaves chopped

PISTACHIO AND TAHINI SAUCE

1 thick slice day-old rustic bread,
    crusts removed

$1\frac{1}{2}$ cups shelled pistachios

2 garlic cloves, chopped

2 tablespoons tahini

$\frac{1}{4}$ cup freshly squeezed lemon juice

$2\frac{1}{2}$ tablespoons olive oil

9 lb coarse sea salt

2 egg whites, lightly beaten

$6\frac{3}{4}$ lb whole snapper, cleaned
    with scales left on

BEET SALAD

Preheat the oven to 350°F.

Place the beets in a small baking dish, add $2\frac{1}{2}$ tablespoons of the olive oil and toss to coat. Roast for $1\frac{1}{2}$ hours, or until tender — insert a skewer into the centers to check if they are done. When cool enough to handle, remove the skins and cut into $\frac{5}{8}$-inch-thick wedges. Put the currants in a small bowl and pour over just enough boiling water to cover. Leave to soak for 10 minutes, then drain well. Combine the garlic, egg yolk, mustard and vinegar in a bowl and whisk well to combine. Whisking constantly, add the remaining olive oil in a slow, steady stream until the mixture is thickened and emulsified. Stir in the currants and season with salt and pepper. Combine the beets in a bowl with the olives and radicchio; season with salt and pepper, tossing well to combine. Drizzle the dressing over the mixture and sprinkle with cilantro. Cover with plastic wrap and refrigerate until ready to serve.

PISTACHIO AND TAHINI SAUCE

Soak the bread in a bowl of water, then use your hands to squeeze as much water out as possible. Place in a food processor with the pistachios and garlic and process until the nuts are very finely chopped. Add the remaining ingredients and process well to combine. Using the pulse button, add $\frac{1}{2}$ cup water or just enough to create a smooth pouring consistency; season with salt and pepper. Set aside until ready to serve.

When you are ready to cook the fish, increase the oven temperature to 425°F. Combine the coarse sea salt and egg whites in a large bowl and stir well to combine. Spread one-third of the salt mixture in the base of a baking dish large enough to hold the fish, then place the fish on top. Press the remaining salt mixture over the top of the fish, packing to seal and enclose (the tail may protrude slightly). Bake the fish in the oven for about 55 minutes, or until the salt has formed a very hard crust. Using a meat mallet, crack open the crust, using your hands to pull off the salt. Peel off and discard the skin, then serve the fish immediately with the pistachio and tahini sauce and beet salad passed separately. **SERVES 6–8**

BAKED SQUID STUFFED WITH ORANGE, HERBS AND CURRANTS

INGREDIENTS

six $\frac{1}{2}$-lb squid, cleaned, tubes, "wings"
    and tentacles reserved separately

$\frac{1}{2}$ cup extra virgin olive oil

1 onion, finely chopped

3 garlic cloves

$\frac{1}{3}$ cup currants

$\frac{1}{3}$ cup pistachios, chopped

$1\frac{1}{4}$ cups fresh breadcrumbs

4 oz feta cheese, crumbled

$1\frac{1}{2}$ teaspoons finely grated orange zest

1 cup Italian parsley leaves, chopped,
    plus extra to serve

2 tablespoons chopped oregano leaves

$\frac{1}{2}$ teaspoon dried chili flakes, or to taste

sea salt

freshly ground black pepper

1 egg, lightly beaten

$1\frac{1}{2}$ lb waxy potatoes, peeled

5 tomatoes, quartered

2 red bell peppers, seeded, ribs removed
    and cut into $1\frac{1}{4}$-inch pieces

$\frac{1}{2}$ cup pitted green olives

1 tablespoon tomato paste

$1\frac{1}{4}$ cups freshly squeezed orange juice

METHOD

Finely chop the little squid "wings." Heat 2 tablespoons of the olive oil in a saucepan over medium-low heat. Add the onion, garlic, currants and pistachios and cook for 5–7 minutes, or until the onion has softened. Remove from the heat and cool slightly, then add to a bowl with the chopped squid, breadcrumbs, feta, orange zest, parsley, oregano and chili flakes, stirring to mix well. Season with salt and pepper, then add the egg and stir well to combine.

Preheat the oven to 315°F. Carefully spoon the filling into the squid tubes, taking care not to fill them too much or they might burst during cooking.

Combine the potatoes, tomato, bell pepper, olives, tomato paste, remaining olive oil and orange juice in a large baking dish and toss to coat. Season with salt and pepper, then arrange the stuffed squid tubes and reserved tentacles in a single layer in the base of the dish. Cover the dish tightly with foil and bake for 1 hour 20 minutes, or until the vegetables and squid are very tender. Serve with the extra parsley sprinkled on top. **SERVES 6**

FISH PILAKI WITH CELERIAC, PINK GRAPEFRUIT JUICE, TOMATO AND OREGANO

METHOD

Put the saffron in a bowl with 2 tablespoons hot water and leave to stand for 1 hour or until deep orange. Peel the celeriac and cut it into $\frac{3}{8}$-inch pieces, then place in a bowl of acidulated water (see note page 107).

Heat $\frac{1}{3}$ cup of the olive oil in a saucepan over medium-low heat. Add the onion and cook for 4–5 minutes, or until softened. Add the drained celeriac and stir to coat, then add the saffron mixture, grapefruit juice, lemon juice and bay leaf and bring to a gentle simmer for 7–8 minutes, or until the vegetables are tender. Season with salt and pepper, then stir in the tomato and olives. Cover and keep warm.

Heat the remaining oil in a large frying pan over medium heat. Dust the fish in the flour, shaking off any excess, then cook for 6–7 minutes, turning once, or until just cooked. Season the fish fillets, then transfer to a large serving platter and spoon the celeriac over the top. Sprinkle with the oregano and serve immediately or at room temperature with a green salad passed separately. **SERVES 4**

INGREDIENTS

1 large pinch saffron threads

$1\frac{1}{2}$ lb celeriac, trimmed

$\frac{1}{2}$ cup extra virgin olive oil

2 onions, finely chopped

2 cups freshly squeezed pink grapefruit juice

$\frac{1}{4}$ cup freshly squeezed lemon juice

1 fresh bay leaf, bruised

sea salt

freshly ground black pepper

3 vine-ripened tomatoes, trimmed and finely chopped

$\frac{1}{2}$ cup Ligurian or other small olives

four 6-oz snapper fillets, skin on

all-purpose flour, for dusting

2 tablespoons chopped oregano

SPICE-FRIED CALAMARI AND GARLIC SAUCE

GARLIC SAUCE

2 thick slices day-old rustic bread,
 crusts removed
5 garlic cloves, chopped
$\frac{3}{4}$ cup extra virgin olive oil
$\frac{1}{4}$ cup freshly squeezed lemon juice,
 or to taste
$2\frac{1}{2}$ tablespoons chopped Italian parsley
sea salt

$\frac{3}{4}$ cup cornstarch
1 cup all-purpose flour, plus extra
 for dusting
$\frac{1}{2}$ teaspoon baking powder
1 teaspoon sea salt
$2\frac{1}{2}$ cups beer
$2\frac{1}{2}$ teaspoons cumin seeds
$2\frac{1}{2}$ teaspoons dried chili flakes
$2\frac{1}{2}$ teaspoons paprika
1 teaspoon freshly ground black pepper
vegetable oil, for deep-frying
$\frac{1}{2}$ cup basil leaves
$\frac{1}{2}$ cup Italian parsley leaves
$2\frac{1}{4}$ lb squid, cleaned, tubes cut into
 $4\frac{1}{2}$-x-$2\frac{1}{2}$-inch pieces, tentacles
 left whole
lemon wedges, to serve

GARLIC SAUCE

Soak the bread in a bowl of water, then use your hands to squeeze as much water out as possible. Place in a food processor with the remaining ingredients and process to make a chunky paste; season with salt. Set aside until needed.

Sift the cornstarch, flour, baking powder and salt into a bowl and make a well in the center. Add the beer and whisk constantly to make a smooth batter. Stir in the cumin seeds, chili flakes, paprika and pepper.

Fill a deep-fryer or large heavy-based saucepan two-thirds full of oil and heat to 350°F, or until a cube of bread dropped into the oil turns golden in 15 seconds. Make sure the basil and parsley leaves are well dried before you cook them. Deep-fry the herb leaves, in batches, for 2–3 minutes each, or until crisp. Remove carefully from the oil to a plate lined with paper towels to drain.

Working quickly, dust the squid in the spiced flour, shaking off the excess. Working in batches, dip the squid into the batter and drain off the excess. Deep-fry the squid for 2 minutes, or until the batter is puffed and golden, then remove using a slotted spoon and drain the excess oil on paper towels. Repeat until all of the squid is cooked.

Serve immediately with the garlic sauce and lemon wedges on the side, and the crisp herbs scattered over. **SERVES 6**

FISH KÖFTE WITH PICKLED GREEN BEANS AND LEMON CRÈME FRAÎCHE

PICKLED GREEN BEANS

Put the vinegar, garlic, allspice, peppercorns, chilies, bay leaf, salt and 3 cups water in a saucepan. Bring slowly to a simmer, stirring to dissolve the salt, then remove from the heat and cool to room temperature. Meanwhile, blanch the beans in a saucepan of boiling water for 2 minutes. Drain well, then plunge into a large bowl of iced water to cool. Drain. Place the beans in a large sterilized airtight jar and pour over the vinegar mixture, pushing the beans down to cover. Seal the jar, then refrigerate for at least 2 days before using. The beans can be stored in the brine in the refrigerator for up to 1 month.

LEMON CRÈME FRAÎCHE

Combine the crème fraîche and lemon zest in a small bowl, season with salt and pepper, then cover with plastic wrap and refrigerate until needed.

Put the currants in a small bowl and pour over enough boiling water to just cover. Leave to soak for 10 minutes, then drain well and pat dry on paper towels. Place the bulgur in a bowl and add enough cold water to just cover, then leave to soak for 10 minutes. Drain well in a fine sieve, pressing with your hands to remove as much liquid as possible.

Finely chop about one-third of the fish into $\frac{1}{4}$-inch pieces and set aside. Coarsely chop the remaining fish and combine with the currants and drained bulgur in a food processor. Add the tomato paste, pepper paste, allspice, dill, parsley and chili flakes and process until smooth and well combined. Season with salt and pepper. Remove to a bowl and gently mix in the reserved fish. Cover with plastic wrap and refrigerate for 1 hour to firm slightly.

Take a mounded 1 tablespoon of the mixture at a time and form into a slightly tapered torpedo shape. Repeat with the remaining mixture, then dust the köfte lightly with flour, shaking off any excess.

Heat the olive oil in a large heavy-based frying pan over medium heat. Cook the köfte, in batches, for 6–7 minutes, turning often and adding more oil as necessary, or until golden and cooked through. Remove with a slotted spoon, then drain on paper towels. Serve the fish köfte with the pickled green beans and lemon crème fraîche. **SERVES 6**

PICKLED GREEN BEANS

1 cup white vinegar
3 garlic cloves, bruised
1 teaspoon whole allspice berries
1 teaspoon black peppercorns
4 whole dried chilies
2 fresh bay leaves, bruised
2 tablespoons sea salt
1¼ lb green beans, trimmed

LEMON CRÈME FRAÎCHE

1 cup crème fraîche
2½ teaspoons finely grated lemon zest
sea salt
freshly ground black pepper

2½ tablespoons currants
⅓ cup fine bulgur
1½ lb skinless, boneless
    whitefish fillets
2 teaspoons tomato paste
2 teaspoons Turkish pepper paste
    (see note page 13)
¾ teaspoon ground allspice
2½ tablespoons chopped fresh dill
1 cup Italian parsley leaves, chopped
1 large pinch dried chili flakes
all-purpose flour, for dusting
½ cup olive oil

LAKE VAN AND THE RARE AND DELICIOUS PEARL MULLET

In Turkey, I've had amazing experiences meeting with perfect strangers. Nowhere more than in Van, in the south of the Armenian Highlands. The big attraction in this part of the world is Lake Van, the largest lake in Turkey, which is a whopping 55 miles across at its widest point. Within the lake are four islands, and when I'm in Van, I'm invited over to visit the second largest of these, Akdamar Island.

My new friend takes me on a ferry ride to Akdamar to see the thousand-year-old Cathedral of the Holy Cross, an architecturally important pink sandstone church erected by the Armenian catholics. The exterior is liberally decorated with bas-relief carvings depicting biblical scenes. From the island we look back over the sparkling lake to the vast, open expanse of land on the other side where farmers are fashioning dried grass into huge round bales of hay. Behind this farmland lies a string of snow-capped mountain peaks. It's a place of dramatic and breathtaking beauty and it's fitting that we finish our day-trip off by gorging on the local delicacy, inci kefali or pearl mullet.

This fish is one of the few that can survive the highly alkaline conditions of Lake Van, whose waters have a pH of 9.8. These critters have been an important food here for a long time — in the past they were eaten un-gutted, or simply salted and dried during the long arctic winters. When I visit, the season for the fish spawning is nearly finished, so we're lucky we can still order some from the roadside restaurant near the Akdamar ferry port. The mullet are cooked very simply — either fried, grilled or baked. In season, the mullet are a popular worker's meal — the fish are taken on large rectangular pans to the local baker, who bakes them in his oven for lunch. Today, ours are deep-fried to heavenly crunchy crispness. The fish are picky to eat, their flesh riddled with fine, sharp bones, but they taste sweet, with a not-unpleasant muddy note.

Afterwards, on the mainland, we stop at the resort town of Edremit to take in the views from the hill above town. It's cool, up high, but the views over the blue, shimmering lake are magical. Around us, local families stoke up fires for early evening barbecues. Women sit with boards on their knees, chopping tomatoes and onions for salad and peeling charred, fat bell peppers. They invite us to share their food later but sadly, we're too stuffed full of fish.

A güveç is an uncomplicated all-in-one baked dish commonly cooked in Turkey. The word *güveç* simply means "earthenware pot," and the traditional shallow clay vessel is sealed and cooked in a tandoor oven, which imparts a magical flavor. This then is the cheat's version, but the flavors mingle beautifully nonetheless.

SHRIMP GÜVEÇ

METHOD

Preheat the oven to 350°F. Heat the olive oil in a large ovenproof frying pan over medium heat. Add the onion and cook for 4–5 minutes, or until beginning to soften. Add the bell peppers and garlic and cook, stirring, for 5 minutes. Scatter with the sugar and drizzle with the vinegar, then transfer to the oven and cook for 15 minutes, or until the vegetables are starting to brown slightly. Add the cherry tomatoes, oregano, paprika, allspice, shrimp and feta, season with salt and pepper, and gently toss to combine. Return to the oven and bake for 10–15 minutes more, or until the shrimp are just cooked through. Sprinkle with the parsley and serve immediately with the crusty bread and green salad passed separately. **SERVES 6**

INGREDIENTS

$\frac{1}{3}$ cup extra virgin olive oil

2 large red onions, cut into $\frac{5}{8}$-inch pieces

2 bell peppers, ribs removed,
    seeded and cut into $\frac{3}{4}$-inch pieces

1 large yellow bell pepper, seeded,
    ribs removed and cut into $\frac{3}{4}$-inch pieces

4 garlic cloves, chopped

1 tablespoon superfine sugar

$1\frac{1}{2}$ tablespoons red wine vinegar

$1\frac{1}{4}$ lb cherry tomatoes, halved

$2\frac{1}{2}$ tablespoons chopped fresh oregano

1 teaspoon paprika

$\frac{1}{2}$ teaspoon ground allspice

$4\frac{1}{2}$ lb raw large shrimp, peeled and deveined

6 oz feta cheese, coarsely crumbled

sea salt

freshly ground black pepper

3 tablespoons chopped Italian parsley

rustic bread slices, to serve

green salad, to serve

GRILLED COD WITH SAFFRON FENNEL AND ALMOND TARATOR

ALMOND TARATOR

1 thick slice day-old rustic bread,
    crusts trimmed
$1\frac{1}{4}$ cups blanched almonds, chopped
2 garlic cloves, crushed
$\frac{1}{2}$ teaspoon ground cinnamon
$\frac{1}{4}$ cup white wine vinegar
$\frac{1}{3}$ cup extra virgin olive oil
sea salt
freshly ground black pepper

SAFFRON FENNEL

$\frac{1}{2}$ teaspoon saffron threads
$\frac{1}{3}$ cup olive oil
2 fennel bulbs, trimmed, halved lengthwise
    and cut into wedges
$1\frac{1}{2}$ tablespoons freshly squeezed lemon juice
$2\frac{1}{2}$ teaspoons superfine sugar

six 6-oz boneless cod fillets, skin on
2 tablespoons olive oil
sea salt
freshly ground black pepper
boiled potatoes, to serve

ALMOND TARATOR

Soak the bread in a bowl of water, then use your hands to squeeze as much excess water out as possible. Combine the bread with the remaining ingredients in a food processor and process to make a coarse paste. Season with salt and pepper — the tarator should have a thick, creamy consistency; you may need to thin with a little warm water to achieve the right consistency. Set aside.

SAFFRON FENNEL

To make the saffron fennel, soak the saffron threads in 2 tablespoons hot water for 40 minutes. Preheat the oven to 350°F. Heat the olive oil in a large heavy-based frying pan over medium heat. Add the fennel, in batches, and cook for 3 minutes on each side, or until light golden. Transfer with any pan juices to a large baking dish. Sprinkle with the lemon juice, sugar and the saffron mixture and season with salt and pepper. Cover the dish tightly with foil and bake for $1-1\frac{1}{2}$ hours, or until the fennel is very tender. Keep warm until ready to serve.

Heat a grill or griddle pan to medium-high. Brush the fish with olive oil and season with salt and pepper, then cook for about 3 minutes on each side, or until just cooked through. Serve with the boiled potatoes and saffron fennel, with the almond tarator spooned over the top. **SERVES 6**

OCTOPUS STEW WITH WINE, SPICES AND CAPERBERRIES

METHOD

Heat the olive oil in a large saucepan over medium heat. Add the onion, carrot and garlic and cook for 5–7 minutes, or until the onion has softened. Add the octopus, pepper paste, tomato paste, paprika, allspice, chili flakes and cinnamon, and cook for 2 minutes, or until fragrant. Add the wine and vinegar and bring the mixture to a simmer, then reduce the heat to low, cover, and cook for 1 hour. Remove the lid and continue simmering uncovered for another 30 minutes, or until the octopus is tender. Remove from the heat, stir in the caperberries and parsley and serve immediately. **SERVES 6**

INGREDIENTS

$2\frac{1}{2}$ tablespoons olive oil

2 onions, chopped

2 carrots, cut into $\frac{1}{4}$-inch-thick rings

3 garlic cloves, crushed

$2\frac{3}{4}$ lb baby octopus, cleaned

$2\frac{1}{2}$ tablespoons Turkish pepper paste (see note page 13)

$1\frac{1}{2}$ tablespoons tomato paste

2 teaspoons paprika

$1\frac{1}{2}$ teaspoons ground allspice

1 teaspoon dried chili flakes

1 cinnamon stick

$1\frac{1}{4}$ cups red wine

$1\frac{1}{2}$ tablespoons red wine vinegar

$\frac{3}{4}$ cup caperberries

$\frac{1}{2}$ cup chopped Italian parsley

SARDINES WITH THYME-PAPRIKA CRUMBS AND POTATO-GARLIC PURÉE

POTATO–GARLIC PURÉE

Cook the potatoes in a saucepan of boiling water for 15–20 minutes, or until tender. Push the potatoes through a potato ricer into a bowl or use a potato masher to mash well. Add the remaining ingredients and stir well to combine; season with salt and pepper. Set aside and keep warm.

Preheat the oven to 350°F. Heat $\frac{1}{3}$ cup of the olive oil in a heavy-based ovenproof frying pan over medium heat. Add the breadcrumbs, onion, garlic, paprika and chili flakes and stir well to combine. Bake in the oven for 20 minutes, or until deep golden, then remove from the oven. Add the thyme, olives and almonds, stir well to combine, and season with salt and pepper. Cool slightly.

Use $1\frac{1}{2}$ tablespoons of the oil to grease the base and side of a $10\frac{1}{2}$-inch-square ceramic baking dish. Working with one sardine fillet at a time, spoon a scant 1 tablespoon of the crumb mixture along the head end and roll up towards the tail. Place the rolled sardine in the baking dish and repeat until all are rolled. Scatter any remaining crumb mixture over the top and drizzle with the remaining olive oil. Bake the sardines in the oven for 20 minutes, or until they are just cooked through. Serve hot or at room temperature with the potato–garlic purée and lemon wedges passed separately. **SERVES 6–8**

POTATO–GARLIC PURÉE

1 lb all-purpose potatoes, peeled and halved

3–4 garlic cloves, crushed

$2\frac{1}{2}$ tablespoons white wine vinegar

$\frac{1}{2}$ cup extra virgin olive oil

sea salt

freshly ground black pepper

$\frac{2}{3}$ cup extra virgin olive oil

1 cup dry breadcrumbs

1 small onion, finely chopped

2 garlic cloves, crushed

$1\frac{1}{2}$ teaspoons sweet paprika

$\frac{1}{2}$ teaspoon dried chili flakes

3 teaspoons thyme leaves

$\frac{1}{3}$ cup pitted black olives, chopped

$\frac{1}{2}$ cup blanched almonds,
    roasted and chopped

sea salt

freshly ground black pepper

24 butterflied sardine fillets (about $1\frac{3}{4}$ lb)

lemon wedges, to serve

HAYAT CADDESI

BALIKÇI DERYA

SWORDFISH KEBABS WITH CELERIAC, ORANGE AND WALNUT SALAD

INGREDIENTS

four 7-oz skinless, boneless swordfish steaks

2 garlic cloves, crushed

1 cup freshly squeezed orange juice

$\frac{1}{3}$ cup extra virgin olive oil

2 tablespoons chopped fresh dill

CELERIAC, ORANGE AND WALNUT SALAD

$\frac{1}{2}$ cup freshly squeezed orange juice

2 teaspoons finely grated orange zest

$1\frac{1}{4}$ lb celeriac, trimmed and peeled

1 garlic clove, crushed

$\frac{1}{3}$ cup walnuts, chopped

sea salt

2 oranges, peeled, white pith removed and
    sliced into $\frac{1}{4}$-inch rounds

METHOD

Cut the swordfish into $1\frac{1}{4}$-inch pieces. Combine in a bowl with the garlic, orange juice, $\frac{1}{4}$ cup of the olive oil and dill and toss to coat. Cover with plastic wrap and refrigerate for 2–3 hours. Soak 12 wooden skewers in water for 30 minutes, then drain well.

CELERIAC, ORANGE AND WALNUT SALAD

Combine the orange juice and orange zest in a large bowl. Cut the celeriac in half lengthwise, finely slice, then cut into very fine matchsticks, adding them to the orange juice mixture in the bowl as you go to prevent them from browning — you may need to add a little more juice to coat the celeriac but take care not to add too much or the dressing will be too thin. Add the garlic and walnuts, then season with salt and toss well to combine. Just before serving fold in the orange slices.

Preheat a grill or griddle pan to medium-high. Drain the fish and thread onto the soaked skewers, brush with the remaining oil and cook the fish, turning often for about 5 minutes, or until just cooked through but still a little pink in the middle. Serve immediately with the salad. **SERVES 4**

SALMON BAKED IN VINE LEAVES WITH GRAPE SAUCE

METHOD

Preheat the oven to 400°F. Working with one salmon fillet at a time, wrap a vine leaf around the middle of each, making sure the seam overlaps on the skin side. Set aside.

Put the wine, grape juice, pekmez and cinnamon in a large ovenproof frying pan and bring to a boil. Reduce the heat to medium and simmer for 7–8 minutes, or until the liquid has reduced by half. Carefully add the salmon to the pan in a single layer, seam side down, then tuck the bay leaves around the fish and scatter over the grapes. Bake in the oven for 8–10 minutes, or until the fish is cooked through but still a little pink in the middle. Remove from the oven and serve immediately. **SERVES 6**

INGREDIENTS

twelve 4-oz skinless, boneless salmon fillets

12 large preserved vine leaves, rinsed well and dried

1 cup red wine

1 cup grape juice

$2\frac{1}{2}$ tablespoons pekmez (see note page 73)

$1\frac{1}{2}$ cinnamon sticks, broken

5 fresh bay leaves

2 cups seedless black grapes, halved

POULTRY AND MEAT

Meat features heavily in the Turkish diet; beef and chicken are widely consumed but really, when a Turk says "meat" he means lamb or mutton. On weekends or long summer evenings, it is not uncommon for Turkish families to pack up their portable *mangal* (charcoal grill), take it to a park or beach and fire it up. Apart from special ceremonies or occasions when a whole animal might be cooked, meat dishes mostly comprise minced or cut-up pieces of flesh cooked with vegetables or fruits, most likely a throwback to the Ottoman era. As an Islamic nation, meat in Turkey must be halal and is always very well cooked.

CHICKEN LIVER KEBABS WITH CHESTNUT PILAF AND RAISIN HOSHAF

RAISIN HOSHAF

Put the raisins in a bowl and pour over $^3/_4$ cup boiling water. Leave to soak for 30 minutes, then place in a saucepan with the soaking liquid over medium-low heat with the sugar. Bring slowly to a simmer and cook for about 15 minutes, or until the liquid is reduced and syrupy. Remove from the heat and cool. Hoshaf will keep indefinitely, stored in an airtight container, in the refrigerator.

Cut each chicken liver into thirds crosswise. Combine in a bowl with the garlic, cloves and olive oil, stir to coat well, then cover with plastic wrap and refrigerate for 2–3 hours.

CHESTNUT PILAF

Preheat the oven to 350°F. Use a small, sharp knife to cut a small cross in the base of each chestnut. Place in a roasting pan and cook for 20 minutes. Cool slightly; then, when cool enough to handle, peel the chestnuts to remove the papery layer.

Rinse the bulgur well and then drain. Heat the butter in a saucepan over medium heat. Add the onion and cook for 5–7 minutes, or until softened. Add the rosemary, bulgur and stock, cover and bring to a simmer. Cook over medium–low heat for 7–8 minutes, or until all the liquid has been absorbed, then quickly fold in the chestnuts. Remove from the heat, cover and let stand for 15 minutes or until the bulgur is tender. Season with salt and pepper, and stir carefully with a fork to fluff the grains.

Meanwhile, drain the chicken livers and thread onto eight metal skewers; season well with salt and pepper. Heat a grill or griddle pan to medium-high and cook the chicken livers for 5–6 minutes, turning occasionally, until charred on the outside but still a little pink in the middle. Serve immediately with the chestnut pilaf and raisin hoshaf spooned over the top. **SERVES 4**

RAISIN HOSHAF
$^1/_2$ cup raisins
$^1/_2$ cup superfine sugar

$1^3/_4$ lb chicken livers, cleaned
3 garlic cloves, crushed
1 large pinch ground cloves
$^1/_4$ cup extra virgin olive oil
sea salt
freshly ground black pepper

CHESTNUT PILAF
1 lb chestnuts
2 cups coarse bulgur
$2^1/_2$ tablespoons butter
1 onion
$2^1/_2$ teaspoons chopped rosemary
$2^1/_2$ cups chicken stock

CHICKEN IN YOGURT WITH CHOPPED GREEN SALAD

INGREDIENTS

$\frac{1}{2}$ cup Greek yogurt, plus extra to serve

2 teaspoons sweet paprika

1 teaspoon ground cinnamon

1 teaspoon cayenne pepper, or to taste

3 garlic cloves, very finely chopped

$2\frac{1}{2}$ tablespoons freshly squeezed lemon juice

$2\frac{1}{2}$ tablespoons extra virgin olive oil,
    plus extra for cooking

freshly ground black pepper

$\frac{1}{2}$ onion, coarsely grated

$2\frac{1}{4}$ lb whole free-range chickens,
    each cut into 8 pieces

sea salt

CHOPPED GREEN SALAD

2 garlic cloves, crushed

$\frac{1}{3}$ cup extra virgin olive oil

1 tablespoon freshly squeezed lemon juice

$1\frac{1}{2}$ teaspoons superfine sugar

$\frac{1}{2}$ teaspoon dried chili flakes

sea salt

freshly ground black pepper

4 green tomatoes, cut into $\frac{1}{4}$-inch pieces

2 small cucumbers, cut into $\frac{1}{4}$-inch pieces

2 scallions, finely sliced

1 green bell pepper, seeded, ribs removed
    and cut into $\frac{1}{4}$-inch pieces

$\frac{1}{4}$ cup Italian parsley leaves, chopped

$\frac{1}{2}$ cup chopped cilantro leaves

flat bread (page 63), to serve

METHOD

Combine the yogurt, paprika, cinnamon, cayenne, garlic, lemon juice, olive oil, $\frac{1}{2}$ teaspoon pepper and onion in a large bowl and stir well to combine. Add the chicken pieces and turn to coat, then cover with plastic wrap and refrigerate for 3 hours or overnight.

Drain the chicken and use your hands to remove as much of the marinade as possible. Heat a grill or griddle pan to medium. Brush the chicken with olive oil, season with salt and pepper, and cook for about 15–20 minutes, turning occasionally, until just cooked through.

CHOPPED GREEN SALAD

Combine the garlic, olive oil, lemon juice, sugar and chili flakes in a bowl. Season with salt and pepper and whisk well to combine. Combine the remaining ingredients in a large bowl, stir gently, then add the dressing and toss to coat. Set aside.

Serve the chicken with the chopped green salad, yogurt and flat bread passed separately. **SERVES 4**

EGGPLANT AND VEAL TRAY KEBAB

INGREDIENTS

2 large eggplants

extra virgin olive oil, for cooking

$1\frac{3}{4}$ lb ground veal

2 thick slices day-old rustic bread, crusts removed, cut into $\frac{1}{4}$-inch pieces

1 onion, grated

2 garlic cloves, crushed

2 teaspoons ground cumin

$1\frac{1}{2}$ teaspoons sweet paprika

$\frac{1}{2}$ teaspoon dried chili flakes

$\frac{1}{2}$ teaspoon sea salt

$\frac{1}{2}$ teaspoon freshly ground black pepper

$2\frac{1}{2}$ tablespoons chopped oregano leaves

$2\frac{1}{2}$ tablespoons chopped Italian parsley leaves

2 eggs, lightly beaten

4 oz feta cheese, crumbled

1 cup chicken stock

2 tablespoons Turkish pepper paste (see note page 13)

$1\frac{2}{3}$ cups canned puréed tomatoes

METHOD

Trim the eggplants, halve them widthwise and cut into $\frac{3}{4}$-inch-thick slices. Layer the slices in a colander, sprinkling with salt as you go and set aside for 30 minutes. Rinse well and pat dry with paper towels. Heat a large, heavy-based frying pan over medium heat. Brush the eggplant slices well with olive oil and cook, in batches, for 1–2 minutes on each side, or until light golden. Remove from the pan and set aside.

Preheat the oven to 350°F.

In a large bowl combine the veal, bread, onion, garlic, cumin, paprika, chili flakes, salt, pepper, oregano and parsley. Use your hands to knead the mixture until well combined and smooth. Add the egg and mix to combine, then carefully work in the feta, taking care not to break it up too much. Use your hands to form the mixture into balls, about 2 inches in diameter, then flatten slightly into patties. Lay alternating slices of eggplant and meat patties in a large round baking dish. Combine the stock, pepper paste and puréed tomato in a bowl and stir to combine. Pour into the dish, then bake in the oven for 1 hour 10 minutes, or until the meat is cooked through. Serve immediately. **SERVES 6**

CLOVE AND PINE NUT KÖFTE WITH WHITE BEAN SALAD AND PARSLEY AND TAHINI SAUCE

WHITE BEAN SALAD

Cook the beans in boiling water for 45 minutes or until tender. Drain well, then cool. Meanwhile, toss the sliced onions with the salt in a bowl to combine well, drizzle with the vinegar, then let stand for 45 minutes or until the onion has softened slightly. Gently stir in the beans, transfer to a bowl and sprinkle with sumac.

PARSLEY AND TAHINI SAUCE

Combine all of the ingredients in a food processor and process until finely chopped. With the motor running, add ½ cup water, or enough to form a thick creamy sauce. Season with salt and pepper, then remove to a bowl and set aside.

Combine the lamb, breadcrumbs, onion, garlic and spices in the bowl of an electric mixer fitted with a paddle attachment. Mix on medium speed for 5 minutes or until smooth and elastic. Alternatively, you can mix the köfte in a large bowl and knead using your hands for about 10–12 minutes until elastic. Add the pine nuts, season with salt and pepper and use your hands to combine.

Take 1 mounded tablespoon of the mixture at a time and form into round oval shapes. Heat 3 tablespoons of the oil in a large, heavy-based frying pan and cook the köfte, in batches, for 7 minutes each, turning often, until deep golden and cooked through. Serve the köfte with the bread and lemon wedges. The onion and white bean salad and parsley and tahini sauce are passed separately. **SERVES 4**

WHITE BEAN SALAD

⅔ cup dried white beans, soaked
    overnight, then drained

2 large red onions, finely sliced

2 teaspoons sea salt

2½ tablespoons red wine vinegar

1½ teaspoons sumac, or to taste

PARSLEY AND TAHINI SAUCE

¼ cup tahini

3 tablespoons freshly squeezed lemon
    juice, or to taste

½ onion, finely chopped

2 garlic cloves, chopped

½ cup extra virgin olive oil

2 cups Italian parsley leaves

½ teaspoon dried chili flakes, or to taste

sea salt

freshly ground black pepper

1¼ lb ground lamb

1 cup fresh breadcrumbs

1 onion, very finely chopped

2 garlic cloves, crushed

¾ teaspoon ground cloves

½ teaspoon ground allspice

½ cup pine nuts

sea salt

freshly ground black pepper

½ cup extra virgin olive oil

rustic bread, to serve

lemon wedges, to serve

A yahni is a stew made with brown onions and a simple stock base, of which there are many varieties in Turkey. This yahni is best served with a plain pilaf, either rice or bulgur, and a fresh green salad.

LAMB, FIG AND ONION YAHNI

METHOD

Soak the figs in 1 cup boiling water in a small bowl for 45 minutes.

Preheat the oven to 325°F.

Heat half of the olive oil in a large flameproof casserole dish over medium heat. Add the onion and cook, stirring often, for 15 minutes, or until golden all over. Remove to a bowl.

Dust the lamb lightly in flour, shaking off any excess. Heat the remaining olive oil in the same casserole dish over medium heat. Add the lamb, in batches, and cook for 6 minutes, turning once, until golden all over. Transfer the lamb to the bowl with the onions, then add the tomato paste and allspice to the casserole and cook, stirring, for 1 minute. Stir in the wine, bring to a boil, and cook for 3–4 minutes, or until reduced slightly, then add the stock, figs and any soaking liquid, lamb, onion and bay leaves. Bring to a simmer, cover with a lid, and cook in the oven for $1\frac{1}{2}$ hours, or until the lamb is very tender. Remove the bay leaves and serve with crusty bread. **SERVES 6**

INGREDIENTS

2 cups dried figs, stems trimmed

$\frac{1}{2}$ cup extra virgin olive oil

5 brown onions, peeled leaving root end intact, then quartered lengthwise

6 lamb rib chops, trimmed of excess fat and halved

$\frac{1}{2}$ cup all-purpose flour, seasoned

2 tablespoons tomato paste

1 teaspoon ground allspice

1 cup red wine

$\frac{1}{2}$ cup chicken stock

2 fresh bay leaves

crusty bread, for serving

THERE IS MORE THAN ONE WAY TO COOK A KEBAB

I've eaten kebabs all over the country. Every region has its own version of the kebab, which in Turkish simply means "cooked meat." Some are so famous they are replicated nationwide, like the spicy, minced Adana kebab. Named after that city, it is a long brochette of minced meat grilled over charcoal. Traditionally the meat for minced kebabs is hand-cut with an enormous, sabre-like knife called a *zirh* — purists claim the finished product won't have the right texture if minced by any other means.

Establishments that make kebabs the slow way using a *zirh* are not so common anymore but do still exist. When I am in Gaziantep I am lucky enough to stumble upon one on Sacir Cardessi, a pedestrian strip cluttered with casual kebab joints. Here they make kebabs using an indigenous fat-tailed sheep called *Helvik* that graze on pastures thick with wild mountain herbs. Great clouds of smoke usher from charcoal-fired grills, over which big meat-laden skewers of kebabs are sizzling. Burly men preside over the cooking, turning the juicy morsels with great care and deftness.

It may not look like it but cooking kebabs is quite a skill. First, a decent kebab needs a judicious amount of lamb fat (about 40 percent) to give it flavor and that unmistakable juiciness. Then the heat source must be carefully managed — the meat must be kept just the right distance away, and then it must be turned regularly so that the fat melts perfectly at the same time. All the while the juices need to be mopped up with pieces of flat bread as the kebab cooks, so they don't hit the coals and cause flare-up. It requires an incredible amount of concentration and experience to get it right. This is grilling elevated to an art form.

Which is why kebabs come in many guises. In Erzurum, I eat cağ kebab, which is constructed of slices of lamb threaded onto a large spit, with a seasoned minced beef mixture layered between to hold it together. The whole thing, which is massive, roasts horizontally over a wood fire and tender, juicy slices are carved off to order. In Malatya, I try the local specialty known as kağit kebab, where slices of meat and vegetables are wrapped in thick, oily paper and baked slowly so all the tasty juices stay inside and infuse everything in their path. In season, they also make an apricot kebab along with the loquat kebab of Gaziantep, and I regret that I am not visiting at the right time of year to try them.

POULTRY AND MEAT 195

PISTACHIO KEBABS WITH TOMATO CHILE SAUCE

TOMATO CHILE SAUCE

2 tablespoons olive oil

1 onion, finely chopped

2 garlic cloves, chopped

2 red chilies, finely chopped

2 tablespoons tomato paste

1 tablespoon sugar

one 28-oz can chopped tomatoes

$1\frac{3}{4}$ lb ground beef

2 tablespoons Turkish pepper paste
    (see note page 13)

3 teaspoons baharat (see note)

1 teaspoon chile powder

1 egg white

1 cup shelled pistachios, finely chopped

1 large onion, grated

$1\frac{1}{2}$ teaspoons sea salt

$1\frac{1}{2}$ teaspoons freshly ground black pepper

7 oz small banana peppers

$\frac{3}{4}$ lb small, firm, ripe tomatoes

3 red onions, peeled and cut into thick
    wedges, leaving root end intact

olive oil, for cooking

TOMATO CHILE SAUCE

Heat the olive oil in a saucepan over medium heat. Add the onion and garlic and cook for 5–7 minutes, or until softened. Add the chilies and tomato paste, and cook, stirring, for another 2 minutes, then add the sugar and tomato. Bring to a simmer, then reduce the heat to low and cook for 35 minutes, stirring occasionally, until reduced slightly and thickened. Remove from the heat and keep warm.

Combine the beef, pepper paste, baharat and chile powder in the bowl of an electric mixer fitted with a beater attachment and mix on low speed for 7–8 minutes, or until the mixture is smooth and slightly elastic. Add the egg white, pistachios, onion, salt and pepper. Mix for another 4–5 minutes, or until smooth and slightly sticky. Alternatively, you can mix in a large bowl and knead using your hands for 10–12 minutes until elastic. Divide the mixture into 12 even-sized portions and use your hands to roll each into a sausage shape, about 6 inches long. Thread each sausage onto a large, flat metal skewer, then press lightly to flatten.

Preheat a grill or griddle pan to medium-high. Brush the vegetables all over with olive oil, then grill, in batches if necessary, for 6–8 minutes, turning often until charred and tender. Remove to a plate.

Brush the kebabs all over with olive oil and grill, in batches if necessary, for about 3 minutes on each side, or until just cooked through. Serve the kebabs with the tomato chile sauce and grilled vegetables passed separately. **SERVES 6**

Note: Baharat is a spice mix used in Turkey, as well as throughout the Middle East. Its exact composition varies, but allspice, peppercorns, cloves, cinnamon, cumin and paprika are common, and in Turkey, dried mint is used too. You can buy baharat from Middle Eastern grocery stores.

This dish doubtless has its roots in Ottoman cuisine, where the inclusion of fruit and nuts in meat-based dishes was not unusual. This chicken dish with dried apricots and saffron is best served with a sprinkling of chopped pistachios or roasted almonds for an extra layer of richness.

MAHMUDIYE

INGREDIENTS

1 cup dried apricots

1 large pinch saffron threads

2 tablespoons butter, chopped

16 small pickling onions, peeled and halved, leaving the root end intact

2¾ lb whole free-range chicken, cut into 8 pieces

⅓ cup golden raisins

1 cup chicken stock

1 cinnamon stick

1 tablespoon honey

sea salt

freshly ground black pepper

1 tablespoon freshly squeezed lemon juice

METHOD

Put the apricots in a small bowl and cover with 1 cup boiling water. Leave to soak for 1 hour, or until softened. Put the saffron in a small bowl with 2 tablespoons hot water and leave to infuse for 30 minutes.

Melt half the butter in a large flameproof casserole dish over medium heat. Add the onion and cook for 6–7 minutes, or until light golden. Remove with a slotted spoon. Add the chicken to the casserole dish and cook for 6 minutes, turning often, until seared all over. Return the onion to the dish with the apricots and any soaking liquid, the raisins, stock, saffron liquid, cinnamon and honey; season with salt and pepper. Bring to a simmer, then reduce the heat to low, cover, and cook for 35–40 minutes, or until the chicken is tender. Stir in the lemon juice, then divide among serving dishes and serve immediately. **SERVES 4**

BAHARAT-RUBBED VEAL WITH GRILLED BREAD, SQUASH AND FIG SALAD

INGREDIENTS

2 teaspoons baharat (see note page 196)

1 tablespoon all-purpose flour

sea salt

freshly ground black pepper

$2\frac{1}{2}$ lb veal rib roast, trimmed

$\frac{2}{3}$ cup extra virgin olive oil

$2\frac{1}{2}$ tablespoons red wine vinegar

3 teaspoons superfine sugar

$1\frac{1}{2}$ lb winter squash, peeled, seeded and cut into $\frac{1}{4}$-inch slices

6–8 firm, ripe figs, trimmed and halved lengthwise

6 thick slices rustic bread

5 cups arugula leaves

METHOD

Preheat the oven to 350°F. Combine the baharat and flour in a bowl, season with salt and pepper, then rub all over the veal to coat on all sides, shaking off any excess. Heat $1\frac{1}{2}$ tablespoons of the olive oil in a large ovenproof frying pan over medium-high heat. Add the veal and cook, turning often, for 3–4 minutes, or until seared all over. Transfer the pan to the oven and cook for 35–40 minutes, or until the meat is just cooked through — the veal should still be a little pink in the middle. Remove the pan from the oven, cover loosely with foil and rest for 10 minutes.

Meanwhile, heat a griddle pan to medium-high. Combine the vinegar and sugar in a small bowl and stir to dissolve the sugar. Set aside. Combine the squash and $\frac{1}{3}$ cup of the olive oil in a bowl and toss to coat. Grill the squash, in batches, for about 3 minutes on each side or until tender, then remove to a large bowl. Brush the figs with 1 tablespoon of the olive oil and cook, cut side down, for 2 minutes or until slightly softened, then turn over and grill for another 1–2 minutes. Brush the bread all over with the remaining olive oil, then grill for 3 minutes on each side or until lightly charred and crisp, then cool. Using your hands, break the bread slices into coarse pieces and add to the squash and figs in the bowl. Add the arugula and drizzle with the vinegar mixture, then gently toss to combine.

Cut the veal between the bones into four even-sized pieces, then divide among serving plates. Top with the salad mixture and serve immediately. **SERVES 4**

EGGPLANT-WRAPPED CHICKEN DRUMSTICKS WITH ROASTED BELL PEPPER AND ALMONDS

METHOD

Using a large sharp knife, make four or five cuts into each chicken drumstick, cutting nearly down to the bone. Combine the garlic, lemon juice, pepper paste, allspice and $\frac{1}{4}$ cup of the olive oil in a large bowl; season with pepper. Add the chicken and toss well to coat, then cover with plastic wrap and refrigerate for 2–3 hours.

Meanwhile, cut the eggplants lengthways into slices about $\frac{3}{8}$ inch thick — you will need sixteen slices in total. Layer the eggplant in a colander, sprinkling lightly with salt. Leave to drain for 30 minutes, then rinse well and pat dry with paper towels. Heat 2 tablespoons of the olive oil in a large frying pan and cook the eggplant, in batches, for 3–4 minutes, adding more oil as needed until golden on both sides. Remove to a plate.

Preheat the oven to 350°F. Place the bell peppers in a large baking dish. Drizzle with 2 tablespoons of the olive oil and sprinkle with the sugar. Roast for 35 minutes, or until slightly blackened around the edges. Remove to a bowl and set aside.

Drain the chicken well, reserving the marinade. Heat the remaining olive oil in the same pan over medium-high and cook the chicken for 2–3 minutes, turning once, or until golden all over.

Take two slices of eggplant and lay them on a clean work surface so they slightly overlap. Place a chicken drumstick in the middle, then fold the eggplant over to enclose. Repeat with the remaining eggplant and drumsticks. Place the wrapped drumsticks in a baking dish, then pour over the reserved marinade and chicken stock. Bake the drumsticks in the oven for 35 minutes, or until cooked through. Add the almonds and basil to the bell peppers in a bowl and toss to combine. Divide the chicken between serving plates and spoon a little of the pan juices over the top. Serve immediately with the bell pepper mixture on the side.
SERVES 4

INGREDIENTS

8 chicken drumsticks, skins removed

2 garlic cloves, crushed

$\frac{1}{4}$ cup freshly squeezed lemon juice

1 tablespoon Turkish pepper paste
  (see note page 13)

$\frac{1}{2}$ teaspoon ground allspice

$\frac{2}{3}$ cup extra virgin olive oil

freshly ground black pepper

2 large eggplants, trimmed

sea salt

3 red bell peppers, seeded, ribs removed
  and cut into $1\frac{1}{2}$-inch pieces

1 tablespoon superfine sugar

$\frac{1}{2}$ cup chicken stock

$\frac{1}{3}$ cup blanched almonds,
  roasted and chopped

$\frac{1}{4}$ cup basil leaves

ROAST GOOSE OF KARS AND A PITI FIX

I'm not big on tourist sights. But it's a long haul to Kars from anywhere and it would be churlish of me to not visit Ani, the celebrated medieval ruins of the old Armenian capital, forty-five kilometres to the north. It's the main, if not only, reason most tourists visit this town. Thanks to frosty Turkish-Armenian relations and the firmly shut border between the two nations that falls to a river right beside Ani, it's strictly on the road to nowhere.

The ruins at Ani are interesting enough and the trip there makes for a pleasant morning out, but truthfully, I'd rather be scratching around the tree-lined backstreets of Kars. Filled with gorgeous old pastel-hued, neo-classical buildings, a legacy of the Russian control of the city that only ceased in 1918, they're a pleasure to haunt.

Kar means "snow" in Turkish and this place gets desperately cold (about –4°F) in winter. This is the season for the goose dishes for which Kars is famous. Geese are reared in the surrounding villages and it is tradition for farmers to kill them in autumn, when they are eight months old. The birds are then salted, dried and stored for winter use. There's a goose market in operation during the winter I'm told, and the birds are expensive, fetching around $35 each.

After a futile search (most places just tell me to come back in January), I finally find a restaurant, which actually delivers on its promise of *kais var*, or "we have goose." The big draw is organic roast goose served on bulgur pilaf with pickles. Once, the bird would have been cooked in a tandoor oven but these days a gas oven does the job spectacularly well, producing rich, gutsy-flavored meat.

I'm not in town long before I discover that a lot of the meat in Kars is renowned for its deep flavor, and then I stumble upon another local specialty I instantly love: piti. A cross between a soup and a stew, piti is a meal served in two parts. Chunks of lamb, tomatoes and chickpeas are combined with rich meaty stock, spiked with saffron, and then cooked for an age in a large enamel mug. To eat it, the cooking liquid is poured over a bowl of torn lavash and the solids up-ended onto a separate plate.

Apart from the forbidding Kars citadel and the striking old Armenian Church of the Apostles, there's little else to do in Kars, but I'm hardly complaining. While I'm in town I turn up for a piti fix daily.

CIĞ KÖFTE

METHOD

Using a sharp knife, remove all traces of fat, sinew and connective tissue from the meat or the texture of the köfte will not be smooth. Using a meat grinder, grind the meat three times, or until very finely minced. Alternatively, cut the meat into $\frac{1}{2}$-inch pieces, then place in a food processor and using the pulse button, process the meat until very finely ground.

Place the bulgur in a bowl and add enough cold water to just cover, then leave to soak for 10 minutes. Drain well in a fine sieve, pressing with your hands to remove as much liquid as possible.

Place the ground meat in the bowl of an electric mixture fitted with a paddle attachment. Add the bulgur, tomato, onion, garlic, pepper paste, tomato paste, pomegranate molasses, allspice, cumin, chili flakes, parsley and cilantro. Mix on low speed for 10 minutes, or until the mixture is smooth and a little elastic; season with salt and pepper. Alternatively, you can mix the köfte in a large bowl and knead using your hands for 10–12 minutes until elastic.

To serve, smear some of the köfte mixture onto the flat bread and squeeze a lemon wedge over it. **SERVES 6**

INGREDIENTS

$1\frac{1}{2}$ lb lamb leg

$1\frac{3}{4}$ cups bulgur

2 tomatoes, coarsely grated

1 large onion, finely grated

2 garlic cloves, crushed

$1\frac{1}{2}$ tablespoons Turkish pepper paste
   (see note page 13)

1 tablespoon tomato paste

$1\frac{1}{2}$ tablespoons pomegranate molasses
   (see note page 25)

$\frac{1}{2}$ teaspoon ground allspice

2 teaspoons ground cumin

2 teaspoons dried chili flakes, or to taste

1 cup Italian parsley leaves, chopped

1 cup cilantro leaves, chopped

sea salt

freshly ground black pepper

flat bread (page 63), to serve

lemon wedges, to serve

BAKED RABBIT WITH CINNAMON RICE AND LEMON SAUCE

INGREDIENTS

2 tablespoons extra virgin olive oil

3 garlic cloves, crushed

$3\frac{1}{2}$ lb farmed rabbit, cut into
    8 pieces (ask your butcher to do this)

sea salt

freshly ground black pepper

$5\frac{3}{4}$ oz thinly sliced pastirma
    (see note) (optional)

3 fresh bay leaves

$\frac{1}{2}$ cup dry white wine

LEMON SAUCE

1 tablespoon cornstarch

2 cups chicken stock

$\frac{1}{2}$ cup freshly squeezed lemon juice

4 egg yolks, lightly beaten

$1\frac{1}{2}$ teaspoons finely grated lemon zest

sea salt

freshly ground pepper

CINNAMON RICE

2 tablespoons olive oil

1 large onion, finely chopped

2 garlic cloves, crushed

$\frac{1}{2}$ cup golden raisins

$\frac{1}{3}$ cup walnuts, chopped

$1\frac{1}{2}$ teaspoons ground cinnamon

$1\frac{1}{2}$ cups long-grain white rice

$2\frac{1}{2}$ cups chicken stock

METHOD

Preheat the oven to 350°F.

Combine the olive oil and garlic together in a bowl. Place the rabbit pieces in a single layer in a large baking dish and rub with the garlic oil mixture. Season with salt and pepper, then lay pastirma slices over (if using) slightly overlapping, to cover the rabbit pieces. Add the bay leaves and wine, cover tightly with foil, and bake for 50–60 minutes, or until the rabbit is tender. Remove the dish from the oven and stand for 10 minutes.

LEMON SAUCE

Combine the cornstarch in a small bowl with just enough of the chicken stock to form a smooth paste. Combine the remaining stock and lemon juice in a small saucepan and bring to a boil. Whisking constantly, add the cornstarch paste and bring to the boil, stirring until the mixture thickens slightly. Remove from the heat and cool slightly. Combine the egg yolks in a small bowl with $\frac{1}{2}$ cup of the stock mixture and stir until smooth, then return to the stock in the pan and, whisking constantly, cook over medium heat for about 3 minutes, or until the sauce thickens enough to coat the back of a spoon — do not allow it to boil or it will curdle. Stir in the lemon zest, season with salt and pepper and keep warm until ready to serve.

CINNAMON RICE

Heat the olive oil in a large flameproof casserole dish over medium heat. Add the onion and garlic and cook for 5–6 minutes, or until softened and lightly browned. Add the raisins, walnuts, cinnamon and rice and cook, stirring, for 2 minutes. Add the stock, season with salt and pepper, bring to a boil and cook for 15 minutes, or until the liquid has been absorbed. Remove from the heat and stand, covered, for 5–10 minutes.

Serve the rabbit with the cinnamon rice, and pass the lemon sauce separately.
SERVES 4–6

Note: Pastirma is a preserved meat made by salting and air-drying beef, which is then covered with an intensely flavored spice paste made from cumin, fenugreek, garlic and paprika. (Prosciutto is a good substitute.)

KURU BİBER
20.00 TL.

POACHED KÖFTE IN LEMON SAUCE

INGREDIENTS

6 cups chicken stock

$\frac{1}{2}$ cup long-grain white rice

$1\frac{1}{4}$ lb ground lamb

$1\frac{1}{2}$ teaspoons ground cumin

1 teaspoon sea salt

1 teaspoon freshly ground black pepper

$\frac{1}{4}$ cup Italian parsley leaves, chopped

4 egg yolks

2 tablespoons all-purpose flour

$\frac{1}{4}$ cup freshly squeezed lemon juice

$1\frac{1}{2}$ teaspoons finely grated lemon zest

METHOD

Bring the chicken stock to a simmer in a large saucepan over low heat, cover and hold at a gentle simmer until needed.

Put the rice in a bowl and pour over enough boiling water to just cover. Leave to soak for 5 minutes, then drain well and return to the bowl with the lamb, cumin, salt, pepper and parsley. Use your hands to knead the mixture together until smooth and slightly elastic, then add 2 of the egg yolks and mix well to combine. Take a mounded 1 tablespoon of the mixture at a time and form them into small balls, about the size of a large chestnut. Add the balls slowly to the gently simmering stock. Cook the köfte over low heat for about 20 minutes, or until just cooked through, skimming off any impurities that rise to the surface — do not let the water simmer too rapidly or the köfte will be tough. Remove from the stock using a slotted spoon and set aside. Strain the stock through a fine sieve and return it to the pan.

In a small bowl combine the flour with 2 tablespoons water and stir to combine. Add the remaining egg yolks, lemon juice and lemon zest and whisk until smooth. Add 1 cup of the hot stock and stir to combine. Bring the stock in the saucepan back to a simmer, then, stirring constantly, add the flour mixture. Bring to a simmer over medium heat, stirring constantly to avoid lumps, and cook for 5 minutes, or until the mixture has thickened. Return the köfte to the pan and cook gently for 3–4 minutes to heat through. Divide among bowls and serve immediately. **SERVES 4**

POUSSINS WITH SPICED WHEAT STUFFING, PLUMS AND PEKMEZ GLAZE

SPICED WHEAT STUFFING

Place the bulgur in a bowl and add enough cold water to just cover, then leave to soak for 10 minutes. Drain well in a fine sieve, pressing with your hands to remove as much liquid as possible.

Meanwhile, heat the butter in a saucepan over medium heat. Add the onion and garlic and cook for 5–7 minutes, or until softened. Add the allspice and cinnamon and cook for 1 minute, stirring, until fragrant. Remove from the heat and stir in the hazelnuts, then cool to room temperature. Combine the onion mixture with the bulgur, chicken and cilantro in a large bowl, season with salt and pepper, then stir well to combine.

Preheat the oven to 350°F and lightly grease a large baking dish. Working with one poussin at a time, fill the cavity with the spiced wheat stuffing and secure each opening with a toothpick. Tie the legs together with kitchen string to secure. Arrange the poussins in the prepared dish, breast side down. Combine the pekmez and red wine and drizzle over the poussins to coat. Season with salt and pepper and cook in the oven for 45 minutes. Turn the poussins over, add the plums to the dish, and continue cooking for 20 minutes, or until the poussins and stuffing are cooked through and the plums are tender. Remove the kitchen string and toothpicks and serve the poussins and plums with any pan juices spooned over the top. **SERVES 4**

SPICED WHEAT STUFFING

$\frac{3}{4}$ cup coarse bulgur

2 tablespoons unsalted butter

1 onion, finely chopped

1 garlic clove, crushed

$\frac{1}{2}$ teaspoon ground allspice

$\frac{1}{2}$ teaspoon ground cinnamon

$\frac{1}{2}$ cup shelled hazelnuts, roasted, peeled and chopped

$\frac{3}{4}$ lb ground chicken

1 cup cilantro leaves, chopped

sea salt

freshly ground black pepper

2 tablespoons olive oil

four 14-oz poussins, trimmed and giblets removed

$\frac{1}{3}$ cup pekmez (see note page 73)

$\frac{1}{4}$ cup red wine

sea salt

freshly ground black pepper

6 large, firm, ripe plums, halved, stones removed

This slow-roasted lamb is terrific served with the bulgur pilaf on page 140, especially with a few handfuls of torn mint leaves stirred through the bulgur just before serving.

SLOW-ROASTED LAMB WITH APPLES POACHED IN POMEGRANATE JUICE

METHOD

Preheat the oven to 300°F. Trim any excess fat from the leg of lamb.

Combine the butter, paprika, cumin, cinnamon, salt and pepper in a bowl. Smear the butter mixture over the lamb, then wrap the leg in foil or parchment paper and place in a baking dish. Bake the lamb in the oven for 6–7 hours, or until the meat is falling from the bone.

About an hour before the lamb has finished cooking, start preparing the apples. Combine the walnuts, raisins, allspice, dried mint and pomegranate molasses in a small bowl and mix well. Divide the mixture among the apple cavities until well filled. Place the apples in a saucepan side by side so they fit snugly in a single layer, then add the honey and pomegranate juice. Cover the pan, bring slowly to a simmer, and cook over low heat for about 40 minutes, or until the apples are tender.

Pull the lamb apart into chunks and serve with the apples on the side and some of the pomegranate mixture spooned over. **SERVES 6**

INGREDIENTS

$5\frac{1}{2}$ lb leg of lamb

$\frac{1}{2}$ cup softened butter

2 teaspoons paprika

$1\frac{1}{2}$ teaspoons ground cumin

1 teaspoon ground cinnamon

1 teaspoon sea salt

1 teaspoon freshly ground black pepper

$\frac{1}{3}$ cup chopped walnut pieces

$\frac{1}{3}$ cup chopped white raisins
    (see note page 134) or golden raisins

$\frac{1}{2}$ teaspoon ground allspice

$1\frac{1}{2}$ teaspoons dried mint

1 tablespoon pomegranate molasses
    (see note page 25)

6 small Granny Smith apples, peeled
    and cored

2 tablespoons honey

2 cups pomegranate juice

LAMB CHOPS BAKED IN PAPER WITH POTATOES, LEMON, MINT AND OLIVES

INGREDIENTS

6 boneless lamb shoulder chops ($3\frac{1}{4}$ lb)

2 tablespoons olive oil

sea salt

freshly ground black pepper

3 garlic cloves, finely chopped

$1\frac{1}{4}$ lb waxy potatoes, peeled and
  halved if large

$1\frac{1}{4}$ lb unripe red tomatoes, cut into
  thick wedges

2 teaspoons dried mint

$1\frac{1}{2}$ teaspoons cumin seeds

1 lemon, thinly sliced

$\frac{1}{2}$ cup Ligurian or other small olives

METHOD

Preheat the oven to 325°F. Cut each chop in half using the natural lines of the meat as a guide, then remove any excess fat. Cut six 12-inch squares of parchment paper.

Heat 1 tablespoon of the olive oil in a large frying pan over medium-high heat. Add the lamb and cook for 1–2 minutes on each side, or until browned all over. Remove from the heat. Working with one sheet of paper at a time, place two pieces of lamb in the center of each, season with salt and pepper and sprinkle over a little of the garlic. Bring two opposite sides of the paper together over the top of the meat and fold several times to seal. Fold the other sides over the meat to form a tight package, then use small metal skewers to seal each parcel. Set aside.

Peel the potatoes and cut them into quarters lengthwise, then place into a roasting dish with the tomato. Drizzle with the remaining oil, scatter with the mint, cumin seeds, remaining garlic and lemon slices and season well with salt and pepper. Toss to coat the vegetables and cook in the oven for 30 minutes, then tuck the lamb parcels in among the potato mixture. Scatter with the olives and cook for another 20–30 minutes, or until the lamb is cooked through and the vegetables are tender. Remove from the oven, cover the dish with foil, and rest the meat for 10 minutes before serving. Serve the lamb in the paper with the potato mixture to the side. **SERVES 6**

ROAST CARROT, VEAL AND LEMON-SCENTED MOUSSAKA

SAUCE

$2\frac{1}{2}$ cups whole milk

3 tablespoons butter

$\frac{1}{3}$ cup all-purpose flour

1 teaspoon finely grated lemon zest

$1\frac{1}{2}$ tablespoons chopped oregano

2 egg yolks, beaten

sea salt

freshly ground black pepper

$2\frac{3}{4}$ lb carrots, cut into $\frac{1}{4}$-inch-thick
    batons

$\frac{1}{2}$ cup olive oil

2 onions, finely chopped

3 garlic cloves, finely chopped

$1\frac{1}{4}$ lb ground veal

$2\frac{1}{2}$ tablespoons tomato paste

1 teaspoon ground allspice

$\frac{1}{4}$ cup currants

14-oz can chopped tomatoes

sea salt

freshly ground black pepper

SAUCE

Put the milk in a small saucepan and bring to a simmer, then remove from the heat. Melt the butter in a separate saucepan over medium-low heat, then add the flour and cook, stirring, for 2 minutes. Add the milk, $\frac{1}{2}$ cup at a time, stirring constantly and bringing back to a simmer between each addition. Reduce the heat and cook the sauce for about 7–8 minutes, stirring often to prevent lumps forming. Remove from the heat and cool slightly, stirring occasionally to prevent a skin forming. Stir in the lemon zest, oregano and egg yolk, season with salt and pepper, then cover the surface directly with plastic wrap or parchment paper to prevent a skin forming.

Preheat the oven to 350°F. Combine the carrots in a large bowl with $\frac{1}{3}$ cup of the olive oil, tossing to coat well. Divide between two large baking dishes and cook in the oven for 40–50 minutes, or until deep golden; strain off any excess oil if necessary.

Meanwhile, heat the remaining oil in a large saucepan over medium heat. Add the onion and garlic and cook for 5–7 minutes, or until softened. Add the veal and cook for 5–6 minutes, stirring to break up any lumps, until it changes color. Add the tomato paste and cook, stirring for 1 minute, then add the allspice, currants and chopped tomatoes. Bring to a simmer and cook for 10 minutes. Season with salt and pepper.

Scatter half of the roasted carrots in the base of a $10\frac{1}{2}$-x-$8\frac{1}{2}$-inch baking dish. Cover with half of the meat mixture and scatter with the remaining carrots, then use the remaining meat to create an even layer and carefully spread with the sauce. Bake in the oven for 45 minutes, or until the top is golden and the mixture is bubbling. Serve hot. **SERVES 6**

VINE-WRAPPED GRILLED QUAILS WITH OLIVE, WALNUT AND POMEGRANATE RELISH

METHOD

Using a large sharp knife, cut through each quail on either side of the backbone and remove the backbone. Cut each quail lengthwise between the breastbones. Combine the olive oil, lemon juice, garlic, cumin and pepper in a large bowl and whisk well. Add the quails and toss to coat. Cover with plastic wrap and refrigerate for 3–4 hours. Drain the quails, discarding the marinade.

Meanwhile, soak 12 wooden skewers in water for 30 minutes to prevent them from burning during cooking.

OLIVE, WALNUT AND POMEGRANATE RELISH

Combine all of the ingredients in a bowl and stir well. Season with salt and pepper, and set aside until needed.

Place a vine leaf on a work surface, trimming off the tough stem end if necessary. Place a quail half on each leaf, pushing the breast and leg together slightly to form a neat shape, and wrap the vine leaf around the quail. Repeat with the remaining quail halves and vine leaves, then use two skewers to skewer two of the quail halves together. Heat a griddle pan or grill to medium-high. Gently brush the wrapped quails all over with oil, and cook in batches, for 10–15 minutes, turning often, until just cooked through — take care not to overcook the quails or they will be dry (they should still be a little pink in the middle).

Divide the quails among serving plates and spoon the relish alongside. Scatter with the cilantro sprigs and pomegranate seeds (if using), and serve with the yogurt and flat bread passed separately. **SERVES 6**

INGREDIENTS

six 7-oz whole quails

$\frac{1}{2}$ cup olive oil, plus extra for cooking

$2\frac{1}{2}$ tablespoons freshly squeezed lemon juice

2 garlic cloves, crushed

1 teaspoon ground cumin

1 teaspoon freshly ground black pepper

OLIVE, WALNUT AND POMEGRANATE RELISH

1 cup pitted green olives, chopped

1 cup walnut halves, chopped

$\frac{1}{3}$ cup olive oil

1 garlic clove, crushed

1 small red onion, finely chopped

$1\frac{1}{2}$ tablespoons pomegranate molasses (see note page 25)

1 tablespoon freshly squeezed lemon juice

$\frac{1}{4}$ cup Italian parsley leaves

sea salt

freshly ground black pepper

12 large preserved vine leaves, rinsed well and dried

cilantro sprigs, to serve

pomegranate seeds, to serve (optional)

Greek yogurt, to serve

flat bread (page 63), to serve

LAMB SHANKS WITH LETTUCE, CHICKPEAS AND MINTED YOGURT

INGREDIENTS

1 cup dried chickpeas, soaked
    overnight and drained

1½ tablespoons butter

16 small pickling onions, peeled with root
    end left intact

1½ tablespoons all-purpose flour

3½ cups chicken stock

4 large lamb shanks, French-trimmed

3 thyme sprigs

1 fresh bay leaf

2 teaspoons finely grated lemon zest

2 tablespoons freshly squeezed lemon juice,
    or to taste

2 baby romaine lettuces, leaves cut into
    quarters lengthwise

MINTED YOGURT

1½ cups Greek yogurt

2½ tablespoons finely chopped mint, or
    to taste

sea salt

freshly ground black pepper

METHOD

Put the chickpeas in a saucepan and add enough boiling water to just cover, then bring to a simmer and cook over medium heat for about 45 minutes, or until tender. Drain well.

Preheat the oven to 325°F. Melt the butter in a large frying pan over medium heat. Add the onions and cook, shaking the pan often, for 3–4 minutes, or until light golden. Transfer the onions to a large casserole dish using a slotted spoon. Add the flour to the pan and stir into the pan juices for 2–3 minutes. Add the stock, a little at a time, whisking constantly and bringing the mixture to a simmer between each addition. Add the lamb shanks to the casserole dish, add the stock, then add the thyme and bay leaf. Cover with a tight-fitting lid, then cook in the oven for 50 minutes. Stir in the lemon zest and lemon juice, then add the chickpeas and lettuce and cook for another 45 minutes, or until the meat is very tender.

MINTED YOGURT

Combine the yogurt and mint in a bowl, season with salt and pepper and stir well to combine.

Serve the lamb shanks with the lettuce, chickpeas and some of the sauce spooned over the top, with the minted yogurt passed separately. **SERVES 4**

Ali nazik is a type of kebab that originated in Gaziantep but is now a popular dish all over Turkey. The addition of sautéed onions is breaking from tradition, but tastes terrific even so. Do try to chop your own meat from scratch and resist the temptation to use ground lamb.

ALI NAZIK WITH ARUGULA AND PARSLEY SALAD

METHOD

Place the eggplants directly over a low flame and cook, turning often, for about 20 minutes or until the skin is blackened all over and the centers are soft. (Alternatively, cook the eggplants on a grill heated to high.) Transfer the eggplants to a large bowl and cool slightly. When cool enough to handle, peel off the skins, removing as much of the blackened skin as possible, and trim the stem end. Transfer the flesh to a colander and drain for about 20 minutes to remove any excess liquid. Finely chop the eggplant, then combine in a bowl with the garlic and yogurt. Season with salt and pepper, then set aside.

Use a sharp knife to chop the meat as finely as you can so it resembles ground lamb. Heat half of the butter in a large frying pan over medium heat. Add the onion and cook for about 12 minutes, stirring often, until golden. Remove the onion to a bowl. Melt the remaining butter in the same pan over medium-high heat, add the lamb and cook for about 20 minutes, stirring with a wooden spoon to break up the meat, until well browned. Drain off any excess fat, leaving 2–3 tablespoons in the pan with the meat. Add the paprika, chili flakes and cumin seeds (if using) and cook, stirring, for another 1 minute, or until fragrant; season with salt and pepper.

ARUGULA AND PARSLEY SALAD

Combine the parsley, arugula, lemon juice and olive oil in a bowl and toss well to combine.

Divide the eggplant mixture among plates, top with the lamb mixture, then place the onion over the top. Serve immediately with the arugula and parsley salad passed separately. **SERVES 4**

INGREDIENTS

$2\frac{1}{4}$ lb eggplants

2 garlic cloves, crushed

$1\frac{1}{2}$ cups Greek yogurt

sea salt

freshly ground black pepper

$1\frac{3}{4}$ lb lamb shoulder, trimmed

3 tablespoons butter

2 large onions, finely sliced

2 teaspoons sweet paprika

$\frac{1}{2}$ teaspoon dried chili flakes, or to taste

$\frac{1}{2}$ teaspoon cumin seeds (optional)

ARUGULA AND PARSLEY SALAD

1 cup Italian parsley leaves, chopped

3 cups arugula leaves

2 tablespoons freshly squeezed lemon juice

$\frac{1}{4}$ cup extra virgin olive oil

DESSERTS

With their fondness for milk puddings, fruit compotes, syrup-drenched cakes, sticky fritters, baklava and the world-famous Turkish delight, the Turkish sweet tooth is legendary. Feasting one's eyes on a street vendor serving the intriguingly stretchy ice cream made using *salep*, or polishing off a selection of baklava, gleaming with syrup and packed with vivid green pistachios, is a highlight of any visit to Turkey. Heady with the flavors of rose, saffron, cinnamon, vanilla, pomegranate, nuts and loads of fruits, both fresh and dried, Turkish desserts are seriously difficult to resist.

I first tried this dish at a trendy canteen in a fashionable precinct in Istanbul where it was served with ice cream — it is one of those dishes that is seemingly artless but its sum is larger than its parts. The trick is to stir and toast the semolina carefully — cook too slowly and it won't toast, cook too quickly and it will burn and become bitter.

IRMIK HELVASI

SWEETENED APRICOTS

Place the apricots in a bowl with $1\frac{1}{2}$ cups water — the apricots should be just covered. Set aside for 1 hour, or until the apricots have softened. Place the apricots and soaking water in a saucepan over low heat. Add the sugar and simmer for 15–20 minutes, or until the apricots are very tender. Remove from the heat, set aside and cool.

Stir the milk and sugar in a saucepan over medium-low heat until the sugar has dissolved. Remove from the heat.

Melt the butter in a saucepan over medium-low heat. Add the semolina and cook for about 15 minutes, stirring constantly, until the semolina smells lightly toasted and biscuity and has turned a shade darker. Add the milk mixture, taking care as the mixture may spit, and stir vigorously until combined and smooth. Add the pine nuts and continue cooking over medium-low heat for 2–3 minutes, or until smooth. Cover the pan and cook for 4–5 minutes, or until very thick. Remove from the heat, then stand, covered, until cooled to room temperature. Fluff with a fork to separate into small clumps, then serve in bowls with the apricots and whipped cream spooned over the semolina. **SERVES 6**

SWEETENED APRICOTS

1 cup dried apricots

$\frac{1}{2}$ cup superfine sugar

2 cups whole milk

1 cup superfine sugar

$\frac{1}{2}$ cup unsalted butter

1 cup coarse semolina

$\frac{1}{4}$ cup pine nuts, toasted

whipped cream, to serve

CHERRY BREAD PUDDING WITH ALMOND CREAM

ALMOND CREAM

1 cup mascarpone

½ cup whipping cream

2 tablespoons confectioners' sugar

¼ teaspoon natural almond extract

CHERRY BREAD PUDDING

2 lb cherries, pitted

1½ cups sour cherry juice

1 cup superfine sugar

butter, for spreading

six ½-inch-thick slices day-old
    rustic bread, crusts trimmed

½ cup flaked almonds, toasted

ALMOND CREAM

Combine the mascarpone, cream, confectioners' sugar and almond extract in a bowl and stir well to combine. Cover loosely with plastic wrap and refrigerate until needed.

CHERRY BREAD PUDDING

Combine the cherries, juice and sugar in a saucepan over medium heat and bring slowly to a simmer, gently stirring to dissolve the sugar. Cook for 3–4 minutes, or until the cherries are just tender and have given up their juices. Remove from the heat and cool.

Preheat the oven to 350°F. Lightly butter the bread, then lay on a baking sheet in a single layer and bake for 10–15 minutes, or until golden and crisp.

Divide the bread among deep bowls and spoon the cherry mixture over the top. Serve with the almond cream and toasted flaked almonds. **SERVES 6**

PISTACHIO-SEMOLINA CAKE

SYRUP

Combine the sugar and $\frac{1}{2}$ cup water in a saucepan and slowly bring to a simmer. Add the cinnamon, then simmer over medium heat for 6–7 minutes, or until reduced and slightly thickened. Remove from the heat and stir in the lemon juice, then cool to room temperature. Discard the cinnamon and set aside.

Preheat the oven to 325°F and lightly grease and flour a rectangular 10-x-5$\frac{1}{2}$-inch cake pan. Combine the pistachios and sugar in a food processor and process into a fine powder. Sift the flour and baking powder into a bowl, then stir in the semolina and pistachio mixture. Combine the milk and butter in a bowl and add to the flour mixture, stirring until smooth. Pour into the prepared dish, smoothing the surface. Bake in the oven for 35 minutes, or until a skewer inserted into the center of the cake comes out clean. Remove from the oven and pour over the cooled syrup. Stand until the syrup has been absorbed, then cut the cake into 3$\frac{1}{4}$-inch diamond shapes and remove from the pan. Sprinkle with the rose petals (if using) and serve.
SERVES 8–10

SYRUP

1 cup superfine sugar

1 cinnamon stick

2$\frac{1}{2}$ tablespoons freshly squeezed lemon juice

$\frac{3}{4}$ cup shelled pistachios

1 cup superfine sugar

$\frac{1}{2}$ cup all-purpose flour

1$\frac{1}{4}$ teaspoons baking powder

2 cups fine semolina

1$\frac{1}{4}$ cups whole milk

$\frac{1}{2}$ cup butter, melted and cooled

2$\frac{1}{2}$ tablespoons dried rose petals, to decorate (optional)

ALMOND MILK PUDDING WITH SUGARED ROSE PETALS

SUGARED ROSE PETALS

1 egg white

36 petals from fragrant, unsprayed roses

1 cup superfine sugar

4 cups whole milk

1 cup blanched almonds

$2/3$ cup superfine sugar

$1/4$ cup rice flour

7 fl oz whipping cream, whipped

2 tablespoons chopped toasted almonds

SUGARED ROSE PETALS

Whisk the egg white well in a bowl. Working with one petal at a time, carefully paint each petal with egg white using a clean paintbrush, then gently dust in the sugar, shaking off any excess. Place the petals on a fine wire rack overnight so they completely dry out. Sugared rose petals should not be made when the weather is very humid. They will keep, stored in an airtight container, between layers of parchment paper, at room temperature for 2–3 days.

Put $3\frac{1}{2}$ cups of the milk in a saucepan over medium heat and bring almost to a simmer; keep warm. Combine the almonds and sugar in a food processor and process into a very fine powder. Combine the rice flour with the remaining milk in a small bowl and mix until smooth. Stirring constantly, add the almond mixture and the rice flour mixture to the milk on the stove. Very slowly bring the mixture to a simmer, stirring constantly to prevent lumps forming, and cook over medium-low heat for 5 minutes, or until thick and smooth. Remove from the heat and cool to room temperature, stirring occasionally to prevent a skin forming. Divide the mixture among six 1-cup-capacity glasses or bowls, then cover each glass with plastic wrap and chill for at least 4 hours before serving.

Top each dessert with a dollop of cream and sprinkle some of the almonds. Scatter with the sugared rose petals and serve immediately. **SERVES 6**

WALNUT-STUFFED FIGS IN RED WINE AND CLOVE SYRUP WITH HONEY ICE CREAM

HONEY ICE CREAM

Combine the milk and cream in a saucepan over medium-low heat and bring almost to a simmer, then remove from the heat. Combine the egg yolks and honey in a bowl and, using an electric hand mixer, whisk until thickened. Pour the hot milk mixture over the yolk mixture, stirring well with a wooden spoon to combine. Return the mixture to a clean saucepan and cook over medium-low heat for 6–7 minutes, stirring constantly, until the mixture thickens and coats the back of the spoon — do not allow the mixture to get too hot or it will curdle. Remove from the heat and cool to room temperature, cover and chill. Transfer to an ice-cream machine and churn according to the manufacturer's instructions. Alternatively, transfer to a shallow metal tray and freeze, whisking every couple of hours until frozen and creamy. Honey ice cream will keep in an airtight container for up to 1 week.

Put the figs in a bowl and pour over enough boiling water to just cover. Let stand for 4 hours, or overnight, then drain, reserving any liquid. Using a small, sharp knife, cut a small pocket in each fig, just large enough to fit a walnut half. Stuff each fig with a walnut half.

Put the sugar, wine and cloves in a saucepan. Add any reserved fig liquid, plus enough water to make it up to $\frac{1}{2}$ cup if necessary (or just add the full amount of water). Bring to a simmer, stirring occasionally to dissolve the sugar. Cover the pan and cook over low heat for 10 minutes. Remove the cloves and add the stuffed figs to the syrup. Bring to a simmer over low heat and cook the figs, uncovered, for 25 minutes, or until tender. Cool the figs in the syrup, then serve with the honey ice cream. **SERVES 6**

HONEY ICE CREAM

$1\frac{1}{2}$ cups whole milk

$1\frac{1}{2}$ cups whipping cream

6 egg yolks

$\frac{3}{4}$ cup honey

2 cups dried figs, tough stems trimmed

$\frac{1}{2}$ cup walnut halves

1 cup superfine sugar

$1\frac{1}{2}$ cups red wine

6 whole cloves

THE CELEBRATED BAKLAVA OF GAZIANTEP

Within Turkey, Gaziantep is fabled for its cuisine. It has the reputation for being home to the best ali nazik kebabs, the best kadaif, the best lahmacun . . . in fact, the best you-name-it. The city is the sixth largest in the country; it's large, modern and vibrant, with a decently preserved historic core. Beyond the city limits are fertile plains producing a cornucopia of produce — pomegranates, stone fruits, mulberries, grapes, sugar beet, wheat and olives, to name but a few. However, the most celebrated crop is the *fıstık*, or pistachio. It's said the pistachios grown here and the baklava that's made with them are the best in the world. If that's not an inducement to visit a city then I don't know what is!

To see how baklava is made is an unforgettable sight. At Imam Çağdaş, one of the largest factories in the city, I am lucky enough to watch the baklava-making process at work. And it is amazing, not least because it is largely a completely manual one. Two men bend over a table heaped with shelled pistachios, sorting them by hand to discard those that aren't perfect. In a room thick with flour, a dozen or so men roll out gossamer-thin sheets of dough using special pins; traditionally pear wood is said to produce the best effect. The flour comes from the Harran Plain near Urfa and is tougher than regular flour, allowing the dough to be rolled so super-thin I can read a business card through it. The rolled pastry is then layered into large round tins and after about the fifteenth layer, minced nuts are spread over, then more layers of pastry. It's cut into shapes using a large knife, then hot sheep's milk butter goes over the top. The baklava is baked in wood-fired ovens (oak wood produces the best result) and it is judged ready when the pastry is puffed, golden and crisp, and the pistachios are bright green. While the cooked pastry is still hot, sugar syrup is carefully ladled over the top — a crucial step as uneven distribution of syrup, or the wrong ratio of syrup to pastry, is said to ruin the finished product.

There are some eleven steps involved in making baklava and it takes up to twenty years to become thoroughly expert in them all. I leave Imam Çağdaş truly amazed at the skill and concentration required to make it and vow not to include a recipe for it in this book. "Authentic" baklava just can't be replicated at home — you have to go to Gaziantep to experience the real thing . . .

DESSERTS 237

CHILLED YOGURT CREAM WITH SWEET TOMATO COMPOTE

SWEET TOMATO COMPOTE

$1\frac{1}{2}$ cups superfine sugar

1 cinnamon stick

2 fresh bay leaves

1 tablespoon freshly squeezed lemon juice

$2\frac{1}{4}$ lb plum tomatoes, halved

YOGURT CREAM

2 teaspoons powdered gelatin

$1\frac{1}{4}$ cups whipping cream

$\frac{1}{2}$ cup superfine sugar

2 cups Greek yogurt

SWEET TOMATO COMPOTE

Combine the sugar, cinnamon, bay leaves and lemon juice in a saucepan with 2 cups water. Slowly bring the mixture to a simmer, stirring to dissolve the sugar. Add the tomato, bring back just to a simmer, then reduce the heat to low and cook for about 50 minutes, or until the liquid has reduced and thickened — place an inverted saucer or small plate over the tomato halves to keep them submerged while cooking. Remove from the heat and cool, discarding the cinnamon.

YOGURT CREAM

Sprinkle the gelatin into a small heatproof cup and add $2\frac{1}{2}$ tablespoons cold water; let stand for 5 minutes until softened. Place the cup in a small saucepan of gently simmering water and heat until the gelatin dissolves. Meanwhile, combine the cream and sugar in a saucepan and heat, stirring to dissolve the sugar, until nearly simmering, then remove from the heat. Stir in the gelatin mixture and cool to room temperature. Add the yogurt and whisk until smooth. Divide the mixture among six $1\frac{1}{4}$-cup-capacity glasses and refrigerate for 3–4 hours or overnight.

Serve the chilled yogurt cream with the sweet tomato compote spooned over the top. **SERVES 6**

SWEET CHEESE PIE WITH OVEN-POACHED QUINCE

OVEN-POACHED QUINCE

Preheat the oven to 350°F. Arrange the quince halves in a single layer in a baking dish and scatter with the sugar and cinnamon. Pour over the boiling water, then cover the dish tightly with foil and cook for 45 minutes. Turn the quince over and cook for 45–50 minutes more, or until the quince halves are tender. Remove from the heat and cool in the syrup. Cut the quince into thin slices to serve, reserving the syrup.

SWEET CHEESE PIE

Combine the superfine sugar and $\frac{1}{2}$ cup water in a saucepan over medium-low heat. Bring to a simmer and cook for 5 minutes, then remove from the heat, add the lemon juice and cool.

Put the ricotta, vanilla seeds, eggs and confectioners' sugar in a food processor and process until smooth and combined. Add the cream and use the pulse button to process until just combined. Add the flour and pulse again until smooth. Set aside.

Brush the base and side of a $9\frac{1}{2}$-inch round baking dish generously with butter. Place a sheet of filo pastry in the base of the dish and brush well with butter (keep the remaining pastry under a damp dish towel to prevent it drying out as you work). Place another layer of pastry over the top at an angle so that half of the sheet overhangs the sides. Brush with butter and continue layering the pastry at varying angles so that the overhang evenly lines the dish. Spoon the ricotta mixture into the pastry-lined dish. Fold the overhanging pastry back over the filling to cover — you can tear off some pieces of leftover pastry, scrunch them up and use them to fill any remaining gaps in the center. Bake the pie in the oven for 40 minutes, or until golden and slightly puffed. Remove from the oven and spoon the reserved quince syrup over the top, then leave to cool to room temperature.

Cut the pastry into slices and serve with the quince on the side. This pie is best served on the day it is made. **SERVES 8**

OVEN-POACHED QUINCE

3 quinces, peeled, cored and halved

$1\frac{1}{2}$ cups superfine sugar

2 cinnamon sticks

$2\frac{1}{2}$ cups boiling water

SWEET CHEESE PIE

1 cup superfine sugar

1 tablespoon freshly squeezed lemon juice

$1\frac{1}{2}$ lb firm fresh ricotta cheese

1 vanilla bean, split lengthwise, seeds scraped

2 eggs

$2\frac{1}{2}$ tablespoons confectioners' sugar

$\frac{1}{2}$ cup whipping cream

$1\frac{1}{2}$ tablespoons all-purpose flour, sifted

$\frac{1}{2}$ cup butter, melted

8 sheets filo pastry

KATMER

VANILLA CREAM

$\frac{1}{2}$ cup whipping cream

$\frac{1}{2}$ cup whole milk

$\frac{1}{2}$ vanilla bean, seeds scraped, or 1 teaspoon
    natural vanilla extract

2 egg yolks

$\frac{1}{4}$ cup superfine sugar

2 tablespoons all-purpose flour

$\frac{1}{2}$ cup superfine sugar

1 teaspoon dried yeast

2 cups all-purpose flour, sifted

1 teaspoon salt

$\frac{3}{4}$ cup pistachios

$\frac{1}{4}$ cup butter, melted

VANILLA CREAM

Combine the cream, half of the milk and the vanilla seeds (if using) in a small saucepan and bring just to a simmer. Remove from the heat. Meanwhile, combine the egg yolks and sugar in a bowl, then add the remaining milk and the flour, whisking until the mixture is smooth. Pour the hot milk mixture into the egg mixture and return the mixture to a clean saucepan, stirring constantly to prevent lumps forming; bring to a boil. Cook over medium heat, stirring often, for 2 minutes, then remove from the heat. Transfer to a bowl and place a piece of lightly buttered parchment paper directly on the surface to prevent a skin forming. Cool to room temperature and stir in the vanilla extract (if using). Vanilla cream can be made up to 2 days in advance and can be stored in an airtight container in the refrigerator.

Combine 1 teaspoon of the sugar and $\frac{2}{3}$ cup lukewarm water in a small bowl, then sprinkle over the yeast. Set aside for about 8 minutes, or until foamy, then add another $\frac{1}{3}$ cup lukewarm water. Combine the flour and salt in a bowl, then add the yeast mixture and stir to form a soft dough, adding more water if necessary. Turn out onto a lightly floured surface and knead for 5 minutes, or until the dough is smooth and elastic. Roll the dough into a ball and place in a lightly oiled bowl, turning to coat. Cover with plastic wrap and set aside in a warm, draft-free place for 1 hour, or until doubled in size.

Meanwhile, combine the pistachios and remaining sugar in a food processor, then process into a coarse powder.

Punch the dough down and turn out onto a lightly floured surface, then divide the dough into ten even-sized pieces. Working with one piece at a time, roll each out to create an $8\frac{1}{2}$-x-8-inch rectangle. Take care not to tear the dough — it should be quite thin and should be well floured so it will not stick to the work surface. Brush each rectangle of dough with melted butter, then scatter with a scant 2 tablespoons of the pistachio mixture leaving a $\frac{3}{4}$-inch border around the edges. Place 1 tablespoon of the vanilla cream, in small random dabs, over the nuts. Gently stretch the long sides of the dough over to meet in the middle and press to seal, then fold over the shorter sides to form a rectangular parcel, about $4\frac{1}{2}$ x $3\frac{1}{2}$ inches, pressing to seal

Heat a large, heavy-based frying pan over medium-low heat. Brush the base generously with melted butter and cook the katmer, in batches, for 3–4 minutes on each side, or until deep golden and crisp. Serve hot or warm. **MAKES 10**

This dessert (along with candied green walnuts, candied tomato and candied baby eggplant) is a feature on the menu at popular Istanbul restaurant Ciya. This recipe is a scaled-back, more user-friendly version — to make it the traditional way requires roasting the pumpkin with calcium hydroxide (or slaked lime).

CANDIED SQUASH

INGREDIENTS

2 cups superfine sugar

$3\frac{1}{4}$ lb winter squash, peeled, seeded and
cut into 2-inch pieces

sesame seeds, to serve

whipped heavy cream, to serve

METHOD

Put the sugar, squash and $\frac{1}{2}$ cup water in a large saucepan and slowly bring to a simmer. Cover the pan and cook over low heat for 30 minutes, or until the sugar has dissolved and the pumpkin has given up its juices. Remove the lid and simmer gently for about $1\frac{1}{2}$ hours, or until the liquid has reduced and thickened. Remove from the heat and cool the squash in the syrup. The candied squash can be stored in an airtight container in the refrigerator for up to 2 weeks.

Serve the squash at room temperature with sesame seeds sprinkled over and a dollop of cream on the side. **SERVES 6–8**

A CUP OF MIRRA IN MARDIN

I was lured to Mardin by the promise of an atmospheric old-world Arab-flavored city, full of historically significant Syriac Christian churches and lovely old homes, many of which have striking decorations carved into their stony facades. They're the color of honeycomb and built into the side of a steep hill, overlooking the Mesopotamian Plain that sweeps on into nearby Syria. Streets are steep and narrow and duties, such as the delivery of goods to the lively food market, are carried out as they have been for centuries, by donkeys.

For most of my stay I dine at the Kamer Vakfi, one of a chain of restaurants established throughout southeastern Anatolia to help women, often in difficult domestic situations, earn a little money and independence. There's a rotating roster of ten women who take turns servicing the menu. If I come early enough I can catch the cook at work, deftly fashioning strips of yufka dough and bits of crumbly cheese into ciğara börek, stuffing köfte ready for frying, or gutting pomegranates.

My other favorite haunt is an antique shop in town where I find myself seriously contemplating a set of old amber-colored prayer beads, finished at the base with a swag of 1930s Turkish coins. Every time I come to lust after them I'm offered a cup of mirra, coffee so thick it's practically molasses . . . minus the sweetness. My relationship with this unique coffee style develops rapidly from revulsion to devotion. Known colloquially as *sahos ayiltan* ("that which sobers a drunk"), mirra is consumed throughout the southeast where it is associated with festivals and ceremonies such as weddings. I soon find out there is an entire protocol that surrounds its consumption. Mirra is made via an elaborate process involving repeated boiling, cooling and the pouring off of sediment; I am told it can take eight hours and three people to make — one to stir the liquid, one to pour in the coffee and another to sing the ballads. It's made in large quantities and reheated as needed. It is always served in tiny cups without a handle and as a mark of respect older people are served first. It's impolite to refuse a cup, as it takes great effort to make, and once the cup is drained (in one swig is considered proper) it must be handed back to the host, never put down. Mirra takes "bitter" to a whole new stratosphere and for a caffeine kick, there's nothing like it on the planet. It clearly impairs judgment too because against my better reasoning, I blow my budget and buy the beads. I blame this on the mirra.

DESSERTS 249

APPLE COMPOTE WITH TOASTED SESAME ICE CREAM AND SESAME BISCUITS

TOASTED SESAME ICE CREAM

$1\frac{1}{4}$ cups whole milk

$2\frac{1}{4}$ cups whipping cream

6 egg yolks

1 cup superfine sugar

$1\frac{1}{2}$ teaspoons natural vanilla extract

$\frac{1}{3}$ cup tahini

$\frac{1}{3}$ cup toasted sesame seeds,
     plus extra for serving

SESAME BISCUITS

$1\frac{3}{4}$ cups all-purpose flour

$\frac{3}{4}$ teaspoon baking powder

$\frac{1}{2}$ cup butter, melted

$\frac{1}{4}$ cup whole milk

$\frac{1}{3}$ cup superfine sugar

1 teaspoon natural vanilla extract

1 egg yolk

1 teaspoon ground cardamom

1 egg, whisked well

1 cup sesame seeds

APPLE COMPOTE

3 cups apple juice

$1\frac{3}{4}$ cups superfine sugar

3 English Breakfast tea bags

2 cinnamon sticks

$\frac{1}{2}$ teaspoon whole cloves

2 lb small Granny Smith apples,
     peeled and halved

TOASTED SESAME ICE CREAM

Combine the milk and cream in a saucepan over medium heat and bring just to a simmer. Using a hand-held mixer, whisk the egg yolks and sugar in a bowl until thick and pale, then add the vanilla and mix well to combine. Pour the milk mixture into the yolk mixture and stir with a wooden spoon until well combined. Return the mixture to a clean saucepan over medium–low heat and cook for about 8 minutes, stirring constantly with a wooden spoon until the mixture thickens and coats the back of the spoon. Remove from the heat and cool slightly, stirring occasionally to prevent a skin forming. Stir in the tahini and sesame seeds, then cool the mixture to room temperature. Refrigerate to chill, then transfer to an ice-cream machine and churn according to the manufacturer's instructions. Alternatively, transfer to a shallow metal tray and freeze, whisking every couple of hours until frozen and creamy. Ice cream will keep in an airtight container for up to 1 week.

SESAME BISCUITS

Preheat the oven to 325°F and line a baking sheet with parchment paper. Sift the flour and baking powder together into a bowl. In a separate bowl, combine the butter, milk, sugar, vanilla, egg yolk and cardamom and whisk well. Add the flour mixture and stir with a wooden spoon until a dough forms. Take a mounded 1 tablespoon of the mixture at a time and use your hands to roll it out on a lightly floured surface to create a $4\frac{1}{2}$-inch log, then cut into even halves. Brush the tops and sides with the beaten egg, then dip into the sesame seeds to coat. Transfer to the baking sheet and repeat until all of the mixture is used. Bake the biscuits for 30 minutes, or until firm to the touch, then transfer to a wire rack to cool. The biscuits will keep in an airtight container for up to 1 week.

APPLE COMPOTE

Put the apple juice, sugar, tea bags, cinnamon and cloves in a saucepan over medium-low heat. Slowly bring to the simmer, stirring to dissolve the sugar, then cook for 5 minutes. Remove from the heat, stand for 5 minutes to allow the tea to infuse, then discard the tea bags. Add the apple halves to the syrup. Place a plate on top to weigh the apples down, then cook over a low heat for 10–12 minutes, or until the apples are just tender. Cool to room temperature.

Serve the apple compote with the toasted sesame ice cream and sesame biscuits passed separately. **SERVES 6**

YEAST PANCAKES WITH RICOTTA CREAM AND HONEY-ROSEWATER SYRUP

HONEY-ROSEWATER SYRUP

Combine the honey with $\frac{1}{2}$ cup water in a saucepan over medium-low heat. Bring to a simmer and cook, without stirring, for 20 minutes, or until reduced and deep golden. Cool slightly and stir in the rosewater. Set aside to cool.

RICOTTA CREAM

Combine the ricotta and confectioners' sugar in a food processor and process until smooth. Add the cardamom and cream and pulse until the mixture is thick — do not overprocess or it may curdle. Transfer to a bowl, cover with plastic wrap, and refrigerate until ready to use.

PANCAKES

Put the sugar in a bowl with $\frac{1}{4}$ cup lukewarm water and stir to dissolve, then sprinkle over the yeast. Set aside for about 8 minutes, or until foamy, then add $1\frac{1}{4}$ cups lukewarm water and mix well.

Meanwhile, sift the flour, baking powder and salt into a large bowl and stir in the semolina and superfine sugar. Add the yeast mixture and whisk well until a smooth batter forms, then cover with plastic wrap and set aside at room temperature for 30 minutes, or until slightly bubbly.

Heat a large, heavy-based cast-iron frying pan over medium-low heat. Add a little butter and swirl to coat the base of the pan. Drop mounded tablespoons of the mixture into the pan and cook, in batches, for 3–4 minutes each side, or until risen, light golden and cooked through, adding extra butter to the pan as necessary. Transfer to a plate and cover with a clean dish towel while cooking the remaining pancakes.

Serve the pancakes warm or at room temperature, with the ricotta cream spooned over the top, drizzled with the honey-rosewater syrup and sprinkled with the pistachios. **MAKES ABOUT 22**

HONEY-ROSEWATER SYRUP

1 cup honey

1 teaspoon rosewater

RICOTTA CREAM

1 cup firm fresh ricotta cheese

$\frac{1}{2}$ cup confectioners' sugar, sifted

seeds from 6 cardamom pods, crushed

1 cup whipping cream

PANCAKES

1 pinch sugar

1 teaspoon dried yeast

$1\frac{1}{2}$ cups all-purpose flour

1 teaspoon baking powder

$\frac{1}{2}$ teaspoon salt

$\frac{1}{2}$ cup fine semolina

2 tablespoons superfine sugar

butter, for cooking

chopped pistachios, for sprinkling

Zerde is a type of rice pudding of which the Turks have a number of variations. Translating as "yellow" in Persian, zerde is light in texture and fragrant with saffron and rosewater. Zerde is an ancient dish that has been served for centuries and is often associated with special occasions.

ZERDE

INGREDIENTS

$\frac{1}{2}$ teaspoon saffron threads

$\frac{1}{3}$ cup medium-grain white rice, rinsed and drained

$\frac{1}{4}$ cup cornstarch

$1\frac{1}{4}$ cups superfine sugar

1 tablespoon rosewater

$\frac{1}{3}$ cup currants

$\frac{1}{3}$ cup chopped pistachios

heavy cream, to serve

METHOD

Put the saffron in a small bowl or cup and add $\frac{1}{4}$ cup hot water, then set aside for 1–2 hours or until deep orange.

Put the rice and 6 cups water in a saucepan and bring to a simmer. Cover the pan, reduce the heat to very low and cook for 20 minutes, or until the rice is tender. Combine the cornstarch in a small bowl with $\frac{1}{3}$ cup cold water and stir to form a smooth paste. Stir the sugar and saffron mixture into the rice and then add the cornstarch mixture, stirring constantly for 3–4 minutes, or until it comes to a boil and thickens. Remove from the heat, stir in the rosewater and cool slightly.

Divide the mixture among six $1\frac{1}{4}$-cup-capacity glasses, sprinkle with the currants and pistachios, then cool to room temperature. Cover with plastic wrap and refrigerate. Serve the zerde chilled with the cream. Zerde will keep, covered in the refrigerator, for up to 4 days. **SERVES 6**

ROASTED PLUMS WITH PEKMEZ SABAYON

METHOD

Heat the oven to 350°F. Halve the plums, remove the seeds and place, cut-side up, in a single layer in a large baking dish. Scatter with the sugar, then roast in the oven for 15–20 minutes, or until softened. Remove from the oven and cool to room temperature.

PEKMEZ SABAYON

Put 4 cups water in a saucepan and bring to a boil. Choose a large bowl that will fit snugly inside the saucepan, making sure it does not touch the water. Away from the heat, combine the egg yolks, sugar, pekmez and $\frac{1}{2}$ cup water in the bowl. Place the bowl over the simmering water and use a hand-held electric mixer to whisk constantly over medium heat for 8–10 minutes, or until the mixture has increased in volume and is very thick — it should hold a ribbon briefly when the beaters are lifted; take care to keep whisking the mixture or it will curdle. Place the bowl over a bowl of cold water and continue to whisk until the mixture is room temperature. Sabayon can be made up to 1 hour in advance.

Serve the pekmez sabayon spooned over the plums and scatter with the pistachios. **SERVES 6**

INGREDIENTS

$2\frac{3}{4}$ lb firm, ripe plums

$2\frac{1}{2}$ tablespoons superfine sugar

chopped pistachios, to serve

PEKMEZ SABAYON

6 egg yolks

$\frac{1}{3}$ cup superfine sugar

$\frac{1}{2}$ cup pekmez (see note page 73)

HAZELNUT MERINGUES WITH ROSE CREAM AND ROASTED STRAWBERRIES

ROASTED STRAWBERRIES

Preheat the oven to 350°F. Place the strawberries in a single layer in a baking dish. Sprinkle with the sugar and carefully pour over $\frac{1}{2}$ cup water, then bake for 25 minutes, or until the strawberries are tender and a syrup has formed. Set aside at room temperature.

ROSE CREAM

Combine the quark, confectioners' sugar and rosewater in a food processor and process until smooth and combined. Add the cream and pulse until the mixture is thick and smooth. Stir in enough red food coloring (if using) to tint the cream pink. Refrigerate until needed.

Preheat the oven to 300°F. Line two baking sheets with parchment paper. Process the roasted hazelnuts until very finely ground.

In a separate bowl, use a hand-held electric mixer to whisk the egg whites until firm peaks form, then, whisking constantly, add the sugar 1 tablespoon at a time, making sure that the sugar has dissolved before adding more — the mixture should be very thick and glossy. Gently fold in the hazelnuts.

Drop mounded tablespoonfuls of the meringue mixture onto the prepared sheets and flatten slightly. Bake for 20 minutes, or until dry to the touch. Turn the oven off and allow the meringues to cool completely in the oven.

Sandwich the meringues with the rose cream and serve immediately with the roasted strawberries passed separately. (Unfilled meringues will keep, stored in an airtight container, for up to 1 week.) **MAKES 18**

Note: Quark cheese is a soft, slightly sour curd cheese — it has a milder flavor and richer texture than yogurt, which makes it perfect for using in desserts. It is available from most specialty grocery stores and delicatessens.

ROASTED STRAWBERRIES

$1\frac{3}{4}$ lb strawberries, hulled and halved lengthwise
1 cup superfine sugar

ROSE CREAM

$1\frac{1}{4}$ cups quark cheese (see note)
$2\frac{1}{2}$ tablespoons confectioners' sugar
1 teaspoon rosewater, or to taste
$\frac{1}{3}$ cup whipping cream
3–4 drops red food coloring (optional)

$1\frac{1}{4}$ cups hazelnuts, roasted and peeled
3 egg whites
$\frac{2}{3}$ cup superfine sugar

POMEGRANATE GEL WITH FAIRY FLOSS

METHOD

Put the pomegranate juice and sugar in a saucepan over medium heat. Bring to a simmer and stir to dissolve the sugar, then continue simmering for 20 minutes, or until almost reduced by half. Combine the cornstarch with just enough water to make a smooth paste and stir until smooth. Add to the pan, stirring constantly, for 3 minutes, or until it boils and thickens. Remove from the heat and cool to room temperature, stirring to prevent a skin forming.

Divide the pomegranate liquid among four or six $3/4$-cup-capacity serving glasses, then cover each with plastic wrap and refrigerate for 4 hours or overnight to set. Serve the gel in the glasses with the fairy floss piled on top and pomegranate seeds scattered over. **SERVES 4–6**

Note: Also known as *pashmak*, which means "little wool" in Persian, this fairy floss (a.k.a. cotton candy) originated in Iran, although the Turks have their own version. Persian fairy floss is available from most specialty grocery stores and delicatessens.

INGREDIENTS

5 cups pomegranate juice

$2/3$ cup superfine sugar

$1/3$ cup cornstarch

Persian fairy floss (see note), to serve

pomegranate seeds, to serve

ROSE AND PISTACHIO SWEETMEATS

INGREDIENTS

$2\frac{1}{2}$ cups shelled pistachios

$\frac{1}{4}$ cup confectioners' sugar

1 cup superfine sugar

2 tablespoons liquid glucose

3 teaspoons rosewater

pink pastilles, to decorate

tea or coffee, for serving

METHOD

Put the pistachios and confectioners' sugar in a food processor and process into a very fine meal.

Put the superfine sugar, liquid glucose and $2\frac{1}{2}$ tablespoons water in a small saucepan over medium-low heat and simmer for about 8 minutes, or until the mixture reaches the "soft ball" stage (this happens when a small amount of the mixture will form a soft, pliable ball when dropped into a glass of cold water). Remove from the heat and, with the motor running, pour the sugar mixture into the food processor with the pistachio mixture, adding the rosewater. Process until the mixture forms a paste, then remove to a large bowl and cool slightly.

When just cool enough to handle (the mixture will still be quite hot), use your hands to knead until it is smooth and pliable. Take a mounded 1 teaspoon of the mixture at a time and use your hands to roll into neat balls. While still warm, press a pink pastille into each, then place in paper cases.

Serve the rose and pistachio sweetmeats with tea or coffee. Rose and pistachio sweetmeats can be stored in an airtight container at room temperature for up to 5 days. **MAKES ABOUT 28**

COFFEE CUSTARDS WITH HALVA PASTRIES

COFFEE CUSTARDS

Preheat the oven to 325°F. Put the milk, cream, espresso coffee, cardamom and sugar in a saucepan and stir over medium heat for 3–4 minutes, or until the sugar has dissolved. Remove from the heat and cool slightly. Strain into a large bowl, discarding the cardamom.

Add the egg yolk to the milk mixture and stir to mix well. Divide the mixture among six 1-cup-capacity ovenproof ramekins and place them in a large baking dish. Pour in enough boiling water to come halfway up the sides of the ramekins, then bake in the oven for 45 minutes, or until nearly set — the custards should still be slightly wobbly in the center. Cool to room temperature, then cover with plastic wrap and refrigerate for at least 2 hours, or until chilled.

HALVA PASTRIES

Preheat the oven to 350°F and lightly grease a baking sheet. Lay a sheet of filo pastry on a clean work surface and brush with melted butter (keep the rest of the pastry under a damp dish towel to prevent it from drying out). Fold in half crosswise, then cut in half crosswise. Brush each piece with butter, then, with the short end facing you, place about $2\frac{1}{2}$ teaspoons of halva along one edge, leaving a $\frac{1}{2}$-inch border on either side. Fold the sides over, then roll the pastry up to form a neat log; do not roll pastries too tight or they will split while baking. Place on the prepared sheet and repeat with the remaining filo sheets, butter and halva until all have been used. Brush the pastries all over with butter, sprinkle with almonds and bake for 15 minutes, or until golden and crisp, then remove to a wire rack and cool. Serve the halva pastries with the chilled coffee custards.
SERVES 6

Note: Halva is a sweetmeat made from crushed sesame seeds or almonds combined with boiled sugar syrup. It is made in block form and sold in slices, and is available from Middle Eastern and Turkish grocery stores.

COFFEE CUSTARDS

1 cup whole milk

1 cup whipping cream

$1\frac{1}{2}$ cups very strong freshly brewed espresso coffee

4 cardamom pods, bruised

1 cup superfine sugar

8 egg yolks, lightly beaten

HALVA PASTRIES

6 sheets filo pastry

$\frac{1}{2}$ cup butter, melted

6 oz halva, crumbled (see note)

$\frac{1}{4}$ cup chopped almonds

INDEX

A

Albanian liver with onion and paprika sauce 29
ali nazik with arugula and parsley salad 225
almonds
     almond milk pudding with sugared rose petals 234
     cherry bread pudding with almond cream 230
     eggplant-wrapped chicken drumsticks with roasted
          bell peppers and almonds 203
     grilled cod with saffron fennel and almond tarator 174
apples
     apple compote with toasted sesame ice cream and
          sesame biscuits 250
     slow-roasted lamb with apples poached in pomegranate
          juice 215
apricots
     irmik helvasi 229
     mahmudiye 200
artichokes, celeriac and carrots in olive oil 107

B

baharat-rubbed veal with grilled bread, squash and
     fig salad 202
baklava 237
beans
     cranberry bean pilaki 92
     fava bean purée with egg salad 24
     fish köfte with pickled green beans and lemon crème
          fraîche 169
     leek and fava bean börek 74
     long-cooked beans and okra 92
     white bean salad with tahini dressing and grilled shrimp 112
beef
     beef and kashkaval pide 67
     pistachio kebabs with tomato chili sauce 196
beets
     beet green, ricotta and hazelnut gözleme 77
     beet pickles in cherry vinegar 119
     beet and yogurt dip 14
     salt-baked fish with beet salad and pistachio and
          tahini sauce 162
bell pepper
     chicken bilber dolmas 138
     eggplant-wrapped chicken drumsticks with roasted
          bell pepper and almonds 203
     muhamara with stuffed flat bread 25

shrimp güveç 173
tomato, bell pepper and rice soup with goat's curd and
     coriander 46
wild greens, freekh and shrimp with spicy bell pepper
     purée 135
breads
     flat bread 63
     pide 85
     simit 73
bulgur
     bulgur köfte with tomato and mint sauce and garlic
          yogurt 126
     bulgur pilaf 140
     ciğ köfte 207
     icli köfte 129
     kisir 144
     poussins with spiced wheat stuffing, plums and
          pekmez glaze 213
     squash tray köfte 133
     swiss chard and bulgur pilaf with spiced onions 141
     tomato, raisin and wheat pilaf 134

C

cabbage, shrimp and rice dolmas 34
calamari, spice-fried, with garlic sauce
candied squash 246
carrots
     artichokes, celeriac and carrots in olive oil 107
     carrot and caraway dip 14
     lemon carrot pickle 119
     roast carrot, veal and lemon-scented moussaka 218
celeriac
     artichokes, celeriac and carrots in olive oil 107
     celeriac, saffron and mussel soup 51
     fish pilaki with celeriac, pink grapefruit, tomato and
          oregano 165
cheese *see also* feta
     cheese and potato filo rolls 68
     dill, lemon and cheese poğaça 82
     fried haloumi with green tomato and celery
          relish 37
     sweet cheese pie with oven-poached quince 243
cherry bread pudding with almond cream 230
chicken
     chicken bilber dolmas 138
     chicken and black-eyed pea manti 83
     chicken liver kebabs with chestnut pilaf and raisin
          hoshaf 187

(chicken continued)
    chicken and pistachio soup 47
    chicken and walnut salad 18
    chicken in yogurt with chopped green salad 188
    eggplant-wrapped chicken drumsticks with roasted
        bell pepper and almonds 203
    mahmudiye 200
    perde pilav 125
ciğ köfte 207
clove and pine nut köfte with white bean salad and parsley
    and tahini sauce 191
coffee custards with halva pastries 265
cranberry bean pilaki 92

D
dill, lemon and feta poğaça 82
dips
    beet and yogurt 14
    carrot and caraway 14
    smoky eggplant 14

E
eggplant
    ali nazik with arugula and parsley salad 225
    eggplant and veal tray kebab 190
    eggplant-wrapped chicken drumsticks with roasted
        bell pepper and almonds 203
    imam biyaldi 98
    red lentil soup with minted eggplant 55
    smoky eggplant dip 14
    stuffed eggplant pickle 118
    turluturlu 108
    yogurt and walnut-stuffed eggplant with tomato and
        pomegranate sauce 102

F
fava bean purée with egg salad 24
feta
    dill, lemon and feta poğaça 82
    homemade pasta with arugula, feta, walnut and herbs 81
    leeks with lemon, currants and tulum 17
    lentil, mint and feta salad with pomegranate dressing 103
    pekmez roasted pear, feta, watercress and hazelnut salad 91
figs
    baharat-rubbed veal with grilled bread, squash and
        fig salad 202
    lamb, fig and onion yahni 193
    walnut-stuffed figs in red wine and clove syrup with
        honey ice cream 235

fish see also seafood
    baked fish with dill butter and raki, roasted tomatoes and
        pine nuts 159
    fish köfte with pickled green beans and lemon crème
        fraîche 169
    fish pilaki with celeriac, pink grapefruit, tomato and
        oregano 165
    grilled cod with saffron fennel and almond tarator 174
    kisir 144
    little fish marinated in vinegar, tomato, oregano and
        allspice 38
    mackerel with onions, apple cider vinegar, cumin
        and chickpeas 153
    salmon baked in vine leaves with grape sauce 183
    salt-baked fish with beet salad and pistachio and
        tahini sauce 162
    sardines with thyme-paprika crumbs and potato-garlic
        purée 177
    semolina-crusted whiting with tomato, pomegranate and
        sumac relish 154
    swordfish kebabs with celeriac, orange and walnut
        salad 180
    tuna in olive oil 38
fritters, zucchini 95

H
haloumi, fried, with green tomato and celery relish 37
halva pastries with coffee custards 265
hazelnut meringues with rose cream and roasted strawberries 257
hummus, warm squash 29

I
ice cream
    honey 235
    toasted sesame 250
icli köfte 129
imam biyaldi 98
irmik helvasi 229

K
katmer 244
kebabs 195
    chicken liver kebabs with chestnut pilaf and raisin
        hoshaf 187
    eggplant and veal tray kebab 190
    pistachio kebabs with tomato chile sauce 196
    swordfish kebabs with celeriac, orange and walnut salad 180
kisir 144

L
lahmacun 58
lamb
    ali nazik with arugula and parsley salad 225
    ciğ köfte 207
    classic manti 86
    clove and pine nut köfte with white bean salad and
        parsley and tahini sauce 191
    icli köfte 129
    lahmacun 58
    lamb, fig and onion yahni 193
    lamb, lentil and mint filo pies 62
    lamb chops baked in paper with potatoes, lemon, mint
        and olives 216
    lamb shanks with lettuce, chickpeas and minted yogurt 222
    lentil, Swiss chard and lamb köfte soup 44
    poached köfte in lemon sauce 212
    slow-roasted lamb with apples poached in pomegranate
        juice 215
    squash tray köfte 133
leeks
    leek and fava bean börek 74
    leeks with lemon, currants and tulum 17
lentils
    lamb, lentil and mint filo pies 62
    lentil, mint and feta salad with pomegranate dressing 103
    lentil, Swiss chard and lamb köfte soup 44
    red lentil soup with minted eggplant 55
    spiced red lentil köfte 13
    spicy lentils with eggs and sujuk 33

M
mackerel with onions, apple cider vinegar, cumin and
    chickpeas 153
mahmudiye 200
manti
    chicken and black-eyed pea 83
    classic 86
meringues, hazelnut, with rose cream and roasted
    strawberries 257
moussaka, roast carrot, veal and lemon-scented 218
muhamara with stuffed flat bread 25
mussel, dill and currant pilaf 149

O
octopus with potatoes, olives and orange-paprika
    vinaigrette 22
octopus stew with wine, spices and caperberries 175
okra and beans, long-cooked 92

P
pasta, homemade, with arugula, feta, walnut and herbs 81
pekmez roasted pear, feta, watercress and hazelnut salad 91
perde pilav 125
pickles
    beets in cherry vinegar 119
    green tomato 118
    lemon carrot 119
    stuffed eggplant 118
pide 85
    beef and kashkaval pide 67
    Swiss chard, feta and sultana pide 67
pistachios
    katmer 244
    pistachio kebabs with tomato chile sauce 196
    pistachio-semolina cake 233
    rose and pistachio sweetmeats 262
plums
    poussins with spiced wheat stuffing, plums and
        pekmez glaze 213
    roasted plums with pekmez sabayon 255
pomegranate gel with fairy floss 261
potatoes
    cheese and potato filo rolls 68
    lamb chops baked in paper with potatoes, lemon, mint
        and olives 216
    sardines with thyme-paprika crumbs and potato-garlic
        purée 177
poussins with spiced wheat stuffing, plums and pekmez
    glaze 213

Q
quails, vine-wrapped and grilled, with olive, walnut and
    pomegranate relish 219
quince, oven-poached, with sweet cheese pie 243

R
rabbit, baked, with cinnamon rice and lemon sauce 208
rainbow chard, vinegared 101
rice
    baked rabbit with cinnamon rice and lemon sauce 208
    cabbage, shrimp and rice dolmas 34
    chicken bilber dolmas 138
    mussel, dill and currant pilaf 149
    perde pilav 125
    rice pilaf 140
    saffron rice pudding 254
rose and pistachio sweetmeats 262

S
saffron rice pudding 254
salmon baked in vine leaves with grape sauce 183
salt-baked fish with beet salad and pistachio and tahini
    sauce 162
sardines with thyme-paprika crumbs and potato-garlic
    purée 177
seafood *see also* fish, shrimp
    celeriac, saffron and mussel soup 51
    mussel, dill and currant pilaf 149
    octopus with potatoes, olives and orange-paprika
        vinaigrette 22
    octopus stew with wine, spices and caperberries 175
    spice-fried calamari with garlic sauce 166
    stuffed baked squid with orange, herbs and currants 164
sesame biscuits 250
shrimp
    cabbage, shrimp and rice dolmas 34
    shrimp güveç 173
    white bean salad with tahini dressing and grilled shrimp
        112
    wild greens, freekh and shrimp with spicy bell pepper
        purée 135
simit 73
soup
    celeriac, saffron and mussel 51
    chicken and pistachio soup 47
    lentil, Swiss chard and lamb köfte soup 44
    red lentil soup with minted eggplant 55
    tomato, bell pepper and rice soup with goat's curd and
        cilantro 46
    yogurt, mint and barley soup 43
spiced red lentil köfte 13
squash
    candied squash 246
    squash tray köfte 133
    warm squash hummus 29
squid
    spice-fried calamari and garlic sauce 166
    stuffed baked squid with orange, herbs and currants 164
sweet cheese pie with oven-poached quince 243
sweet tahini spirals 61
Swiss chard and bulgur pilaf with spiced onions 141
Swiss chard, feta and golden raisin pide 67
swordfish kebabs with celeriac, orange and
    walnut salad 180

T
tahini spirals, sweet 61
topik 101
tuna
    kisir 144
    tuna in olive oil 38
turluturlu 108

V
vanilla cream 244
veal
    baharat-rubbed veal with grilled bread, squash and
        fig salad 202
    eggplant and veal tray kebab 190
    roast carrot, veal and lemon-scented moussaka 218
vegetables with barley and spiced yogurt 115
vinegared rainbow chard 101
vine-wrapped grilled quails with olive, walnut and
    pomegranate relish 219

W
walnut-stuffed figs in red wine and clove syrup with honey
    ice cream 235
white bean salad with tahini dressing and grilled shrimp 112
wild greens, freekh and shrimp with bell pepper
    purée 135

Y
yeast pancakes with ricotta cream and honey-rosewater
    syrup 253
yogurt
    bulgur köfte with tomato and mint sauce and garlic
        yogurt 126
    chicken in yogurt with green chopped salad 188
    chilled yogurt cream with sweet tomato compôte 238
    tomato, pomegranate and mint salad with saffron
        labneh 116
    vegetables with barley and spiced yogurt 115
    yogurt, mint and barley soup 43
    yogurt and walnut-stuffed eggplant with tomato and
        pomegranate sauce 102

Z
zerde 254
zucchini fritters 95

ACKNOWLEDGMENTS

Mist destek na hên lêdan

("You cannot clap with one hand") – Kurdish proverb

Many have had a hand in the making of this book, some wittingly and others not so!

First and most important, I would like to thank the boys in my life, Andrew and Harry, for so graciously tolerating my extended absences as I prowled around Turkey. To my fabulous photography team — Amanda McLauchlan, Aimee Jones and Anna Shaw — a big *teşekkür ederim*; the book is so beautiful because of your fabulous work. Hugh Ford, Livia Caiazzo and Jacqueline Blanchard, thank you for always being so wonderful to work with and endlessly patient to boot, I salute you!

To all the team at Murdoch Books, both past and present, I am beyond grateful for your vision and endless encouragement over many years of association: special thanks to Kay Scarlett, Jane Lawson, Vivien Valk, Kylie Walker, Anneka Manning and Juliet Rogers.

Finally I would like to acknowledge the help of numerous others, too many to name, who have assisted this project in myriad ways, from New Zealand to Sydney and all over Turkey — you've variously aided, abetted, advised, supported, fed and cheered me from the sidelines (and made me tea and sold me kilims!) — a heartfelt thanks to you all.